QUEEN ELIZABETH
THE QUEEN MOTHER
AT CLARENCE HOUSE

QUEEN ELIZABETH THE QUEEN MOTHER AT CLARENCE HOUSE

John Cornforth

MICHAEL JOSEPH

LONDON

in association with

THE ROYAL COLLECTION

MICHAEL JOSEPH LTD
in association with THE ROYAL COLLECTION
Published by the Penguin Group

Penguin Books Limited
27 Wrights Lane, London W8 5TZ
Viking Penguin Inc, 375 Hudson Street, New York, New York 10014, USA
Penguin Books Australia Ltd, Ringwood, Victoria, Australia
Penguin Books Canada Ltd, 10 Alcorn Avenue, Toronto, Ontario, Canada M4V 3B2
Penguin Books (NZ) Ltd, 182–190 Wairau Road, Auckland 10, New Zealand

Penguin Books, Registered Offices: Harmondsworth, Middlesex, England

First published 1996
Copyright © text The Royal Collection and John Cornforth 1996.
Copyright © photographs The Royal Collection 1996.

The specially commissioned photographs of Clarence House are
by Mark Fiennes and those of the pictures and objects are by Stephen Chapman.
The photograph of Queen Elizabeth The Queen Mother
on the jacket and frontispiece is by Anthony Crickmay.

Design and production in association with Book Production Consultants plc, Cambridge
Colour reproduction by Jade Repro, Braintree, Essex
Printed in Great Britain by Butler & Tanner Ltd, Frome and London

A CIP catalogue record for this book is available from the British Library

ISBN 0 7181 4191 1

CONTENTS

ACKNOWLEDGEMENTS

MANY PEOPLE have helped me in the preparation of this book, but, of course, my first and most important acknowledgement is to Her Majesty Queen Elizabeth The Queen Mother. Not only has she sanctioned the idea but has actively supported it, through talking to me on several occasions and taking me all over the house. She first talked to me about Clarence House sixteen years ago when I wrote two articles for *Country Life* at the suggestion of the Duke of Grafton.

At Clarence House I have been greatly helped by Sir Alastair Aird, Queen Elizabeth's Private Secretary, who has taken great trouble over all the arrangements and made many useful suggestions.

Mr William Tallon, the Steward and Page of the Backstairs, has produced early photographs and revealed clues on the backs of pictures.

The book has been commissioned by the Royal Collection Trust and invaluable guidance at every stage has come from its staff, in particular from Hugh Roberts, the Director, who has steered the project along and commented on the text at various stages. He, his predecessors, Sir Oliver Millar and Sir Geoffrey de Bellaigue, and his colleagues Christopher Lloyd and Jonathan Marsden have all provided information about objects at Clarence House and in the Royal Collection; and Caroline Paybody has eased my path. Also I have been helped by the Hon. Mrs Roberts and Miss Frances Dimond.

Among others who have helped me with questions and advice have been Mrs Chloë Blackburn, Mrs Humphrey Brooke, Tom Campbell, Howard Coutts, David Fraser-Jenkins, Philippa Glanville, Ian Gow, James Holloway, Jessie McNab, Sarah Medlam, Lady Penn, Sir Adam and Lady Ridley, and Lucy Wood.

I am most grateful to Mark Fiennes and his assistant Jeremy Hilder, who worked like demons to produce such a fine set of transparencies of the interior, and to Stephen Chapman and his assistant, Dominic Brown, who photographed almost all the paintings and other objects in a second compressed campaign.

Finally Tony Littlechild, Roz Williams, Jim Reader and Tim McPhee at Book Production Consultants made the book rise even quicker than a soufflé.

INTRODUCTION

WHEN DRIVING ALONG the Mall or walking in St James's Park it is almost second nature to look to see if the Royal Standards are flying over Buckingham Palace and Clarence House – and it is always oddly reassuring to find that they are. However probably few people can read the Standard of Her Majesty Queen Elizabeth The Queen Mother, and even fewer have any idea of the character of the interior of Clarence House or realize what a remarkable place it has become and what a special atmosphere Queen Elizabeth has created there during the past forty years. Yet both the Standard and the rooms tell stories that intertwine.

Queen Elizabeth's arms (1) are, in heralds' language:

Within the Garter ensigned with the Royal Crown, the Arms of the United Kingdom of Great Britain and Ireland, impaling quarterly: 1st and 4th (for Lyon) Argent, a lion rampant azure armed and langued gules, within a double tressure flory counter flory of the second; 2nd and 3rd (for Bowes) Ermine, three bows, strings palewise proper.

1. *The Arms of Her Majesty Queen Elizabeth The Queen Mother.*

In lay language, on the left half of the shield they show the Royal Arms; the right half in the top left and bottom right corners displays the arms of the Lyon family, Earls of Strathmore, of Glamis Castle in Forfar; and in the top right and bottom left corners those of the Bowes family of Streatlam Castle and Gibside in Co. Durham and St Paul's Walden Bury in Hertfordshire, whose heiress the 9th Earl of Strathmore married in 1767.

At the same time the accidents of heraldic history provide a contrast between the rich colours of the Royal Arms and the cool blue, silver and black of

2. An Attic red-figure vase, 5th century BC, *and Sèvres huntsmen in the Library.*

Bowes-Lyon. Queen Elizabeth's arms signify her descent from Sir John Lyon of Forteviot, who was granted Glamis by King Robert II of Scotland in 1372, and the alliance between the House of Windsor and that ancient Scottish line.

Today heraldic language is not widely read and to some people it is as unintelligible as Arabic or Chinese script, but here it leads very clearly into the house that has come to tell a story of Queen Elizabeth's life through her pictures and objects, from her very first acquisition made at the age of eight (26). While the rooms cannot add up to a complete, balanced biography, they reflect her background and upbringing. In particular they reveal the way that she was taught to look at things as a child, the events of her life, especially her years as Queen and the tensions and burdens of the war years, and many of her interests, enthusiasms and her friendships. They also reflect the lives of her forebears.

Over the years the rooms at Clarence House have become very full but there is no sense of them having settled into a rigid, final form, because pictures and sculptures continue to arrive and need to be found a home. Objects that appear to have talked to each other on a table for decades suddenly have to make room for new neighbours that may sometimes surprise them (60). Pictures rest hopefully on chairs, in corners (86), or lean rather perilously against busts or by plants while waiting for a permanent place. Pieces of sculpture perch on a variety of stands and little tables (87). However a picture in a stack does not mean it is forgotten: the stacks are clearly rearranged to reveal particular pictures, sometimes to shock or tease, and sometimes to compliment a friend who may find his work promoted to an easel. Almost always there are gaps on walls, because Queen Elizabeth is a generous lender to exhibitions. Thus the rooms are not static or on parade, but have a remarkable sense of the continuing life of someone who has great visual pleasure in pictures and objects and enjoys their associations with her family, friends and events in her life.

3. *A mother-of-pearl casket with silver mounts and crystal feet made at Torgau, about 1570, maker's mark LB. Given to Queen Elizabeth by John Brown and Co. when she launched the liner named after her on 27 September 1938.*

It is the *grouping* of pictures and objects that is the key here, because Queen Elizabeth appears to think about rooms in terms of how things form compositions within them. Whereas some people (particularly those interested in decoration) see rooms as complete compositions, not liking individual objects to distract from the whole, and others concentrate on individual objects, with little eye for their relationship to one another or their setting (as can happen with collectors), at Clarence House several of the rooms seem to build up from separate compositions of pictures and objects, with flowers and plants also playing their part.

The result may be confusing to the eye of the camera, which often seems to call for simplification and thinning out in a room, and to those whose eyes are unconsciously influenced by interior photography, yet it is very satisfying to those who

4. *A triptych with engraved glass panels by Laurence Whistler to hold the list of Queen Elizabeth's engagements. It was given to Her Majesty by Major T.C. Harvey, Queen Elizabeth's Private Secretary in the early 1950s.*

appreciate objects visually and historically, because it encourages them to look closely and enjoy all the elements. Pictures are tied to chimneypieces by the symmetrical arrangements of objects, but then there are occasional breaks in the symmetry (88). Corners of rooms are arranged so that they become still lifes (86), while the tops of tables are turned into compositions with sculpture and masses of photographs (121). Some of the juxtapositions are intended to be surprising and therefore stimulating; in others chance has played a part (108). Thus one wants to linger in the rooms and absorb all that they have to say.

What is most unusual is that there is no sense of a break between the past and the present, with the death of Queen Victoria making a great divide. Not only is it rare for an English collection with a strong historical element to contain so many 20th-century works of art,

5. *Two of a set of four silver-gilt dessert stands in the form of trochus shells made by Leslie Durbin in 1959 and presented to Queen Elizabeth when she opened the Kariba Dam in 1960.*

but the historical thread comes up to the present day quite naturally in painting, sculpture and also plate, often striking sparks along the way. Regency plate by Paul Storr and recent pieces by Leslie Durbin (5), for instance, are rarely seen in use together, but here they are (94).

It is this many-layered approach that makes the rooms so rare and so fascinating. To be taken round for the first time is an overwhelming experience. There is such a wide range of objects, from a Greek pot dating from the 5th century BC (2), or a Roman bust, to Florentine Madonnas (24,118) and paintings by Millais (83), Monet (89) and John Bratby, and taking in a 16th-century German mother-of-pearl casket (3) or a triptych to hold the list of Queen Elizabeth's engagements with engraved panels by Laurence Whistler (4). It is not only the variety, but the range of reasons for pictures and objects being there that is so intriguing; and a great many of them seem to call out, wanting to explain why.

Since there is no formal catalogue for the house with detailed histories of objects or dates and accounts of acquisitions (just working inventories compiled by Christie's and card indexes covering some purchases made after 1937 and before 1952), only Queen Elizabeth can be the guide to her house, explaining where things came from, when and why. Over the years friends have urged her to set that information down on paper. This is the first attempt to make a record of the house as it has developed over the past forty years. Hopefully what is illustrated here gives a hint of its character, but I suspect that even Her Majesty's close friends will not have seen everything and may be surprised by aspects of the story that the rooms and their contents tell. Thus it is a very great privilege not only to have been allowed to make this survey but to have been encouraged to do so by Her Majesty.

One reason why the contents of the house make so strong an impression is that the rooms are surprisingly simple in terms of architecture and decoration. There is no dramatic spatial planning leading off an impressive staircase; there are no state rooms; nor is there even much architectural gilding, just a little lining out; and only Queen Elizabeth's Sitting Room (119) is hung with damask. The interior reflects the postwar history of the house, since it was restored as the London house for Princess Elizabeth and the Duke of Edinburgh on their marriage. Money was tight in the late 1940s and the house was much more simply decorated than it would be today. It had been newly done when Queen Elizabeth went to live there and the rooms have kept a great deal of that character, with plain painted walls and very little pattern.

On the other hand when Queen Elizabeth is in residence, the rooms in use are full of flowers and plants, and their boldness and freedom of arrangement bring the house to life, making every day seem a special occasion.

The simplicity of decoration strikes me as having a possible Scottish aspect. Large Scottish houses are often sparing in their display, happily placing very fine things in simpler settings than would be usual in England, and I wonder whether it is too much to see that spirit, albeit unconsciously, present in Clarence House. It is a house in which objects, rather than architectural design or decoration, are dominant, and that explains the shape of this book, most of which is in the form of a leisurely tour.

Indeed it is so easy to get absorbed in the pictures, furniture and china, that only the stamp of the sentries' feet and the regular bursts of the military bands escorting the guards in the Mall remind one where one is.

CLARENCE HOUSE
AND ITS OWNERS

CLARENCE HOUSE is part of that densely knit enclave of London adjoining St James's Palace where the two grandest buildings (which in any other city would be called palaces) owe their existence to subjects of Queen Victoria. The 1st Duke of Sutherland completed the house begun by the Duke of York, the brother of King George IV, and now known as Lancaster House. (This led Queen Victoria to make a famous quip to her Mistress of the Robes about coming from her house to your palace.) His second son, Lord Francis Egerton, later 1st Earl of Ellesmere, rebuilt Bridgewater House overlooking St James's Park. Facing Lancaster House is the arcade of Hawksmoor's stables and behind the latter is Cleveland Row with some of the narrowest houses in central London.

It is an enclave that conveys a sense of having been rebuilt again and again over the centuries, with Clarence House playing third architectural fiddle to both Lancaster and Bridgewater Houses. That is partly a matter of scale and design and partly a matter of material: stucco as opposed to Bath and Portland stones. Stucco gives Clarence House a crisp friendliness that the stone houses lack, but also disguises an unbelievable amount of make-do and mend over the past 300 years.

Today the main elevation of Clarence House faces south, looking towards the Mall and St James's Park. In doing so it joins the grand parade of Lancaster House, St James's Palace and Marlborough House (6), but that is a comparatively recent development. Before the 1870s the main entrance front was the west elevation (11) looking on to what had become the side wall of Lancaster House. This was because the old house faced west, at right angles to St James's Palace. John Nash followed that line in the 1820s and indeed incorporated some of its late-17th-century walls, so that they influenced the length and depth of his block.

The Duke of Clarence, the third son of King George III, had been granted apartments in the old house, but it was into bachelor accommodation that he and Mrs Jordan and their increasingly large family squeezed when they were not at Bushy

6. *An aerial view of Clarence House from the south-west, with Lancaster House on the left,*
St James's Palace to the east and north, and Marlborough House further to the east.

Park. In 1806–1809 some more-than-necessary improvements were made because
by 1807 the Duke and Mrs Jordan had five sons and five daughters. All seemed
settled with the ménage until 1810–11, when talk of separation began.

At that stage the Duke began to think about a legitimate heir as a means of
getting a regular allowance from Parliament, although it was not yet a matter of
national significance because the Prince Regent's daughter, Princess Charlotte, was
growing up. In 1816, however, she married Prince Leopold, and then came the
blow of her death in childbirth. The Duke was still not heir to the throne (because
the Duke of York was alive), but in 1818, partly to strengthen the succession,
both he and his younger brother, the Duke of Kent, married German princesses
at a double ceremony. For a time the Duke and Duchess of Clarence went to

7. *A detail of Kip's bird's-eye view of c.1712 showing St James's Palace and the site of Clarence House, which incorporates elements from the structures immediately to the west of the Palace.*

Hanover to save money, but after they returned the old accommodation seemed inadequate for their new position. Consequently in 1824 the Duke asked King George IV to make improvements at Clarence House. In 1825 Nash produced plans for an economical remodelling, but, as invariably happened as a result of his carelessness, costs rose. By the end of 1827 the structural work had cost more than £20,000, over twice the original estimate.

Nash designed a new west-facing front range with a double portico for the central bays. The only photograph of this appears to be one taken in 1861 for Queen Victoria when she had a record made of the houses of her mother, the Duchess of Kent, who had recently died (11).

However, no money or thought was spent on designing a proper south front to the house, which, as can be seen in a watercolour of 1861 by Joseph Nash (8), consisted of the present left-hand bay and a three-bay extension to the east that was four storeys high and was set back by one bay, from the line of the left bay. To the right of that was a two-bay, two-storey building that filled the gap between the house and the Palace.

Nash provided a central Entrance Hall, with a Dining Room to the north and a Breakfast Room to the south, with a broad corridor running from north to south behind the front rooms. The site was too shallow and funds too restricted to provide a grand staircase, although the two Drawing Rooms were on the first floor, over the Dining Room and the Entrance Hall, with the staircase at the north end of the corridor.

When the Duke succeeded his brother in 1830 as King William IV, he and Queen Adelaide did not move to the new Buckingham Palace at the end of the Mall but continued to live in the house. After the King's death in 1837, Queen Adelaide

8. *The south side of Clarence House in 1861, a watercolour by Joseph Nash.*

9. *The south side of Clarence House from the garden.*

10. *The west front of Clarence House from Stable Yard with Lancaster House on the right.*

moved to Marlborough House, and Clarence House was then given to Princess Augusta, George III's eldest unmarried daughter; and after her death in 1840 to Queen Victoria's mother, the Duchess of Kent, who was deeply offended at being moved out of Buckingham Palace.

As part of the record made after her death, there are four views painted by James Roberts in 1861. They are of the Dining Room (13), the Duchess's Sitting Room (16), the Drawing Room (14) and the Duchess's Bedroom. That of the Dining Room is of interest, because it shows what a plain room it was: the coved cornice was its only feature. The Drawing Room, which is the north section of the present room, had a coved and fluted cornice, but there is insufficient detail in the watercolour to show whether the flutes were enriched as they are today. The ceiling, however, was plain. The pale blue walls were lined out with bright gilt fillets, like those which survive in the Duchess's sitting room at Frogmore. Her Sitting Room at Clarence House occupied the same position as Queen Elizabeth's, but it was a different room: the chimneypiece was on the south end wall, where the big window is today; there was a window on the east wall that disappeared when the south end of the house was rebuilt in the 1870s; and there were three windows on the west wall, instead of the present two. The upholstery was of the same pattern as in the Drawing Room.

In 1866, five years after the Duchess's death, the house was allotted to the Duke of Edinburgh, the second son of Queen Victoria. However, in 1874 when he married the Grand Duchess Marie Alexandrovna, the only daughter of Tsar Alexander II, he felt the house was unworthy of her. With the aid of a builder, Charles Waller, but without an architect, the house was enlarged and 'turned round'. It was then

11. Above *The west front with Nash's double portico, photographed in 1861.*
12. Right *Sentries outside Clarence House.*

that it became south-facing with the house built out to the line of the Morning Room at the southwest corner and carried across to link up with the Palace (9), so providing three more rooms on both the ground and first floors. A new portico was constructed to protect the main entrance, which was moved from the open west side to behind the gates, with Nash's long corridor becoming the Hall. This explains why the south front is so far from being symmetrical and full of inconsistencies. The Duke also built an extra storey over the

13. Top   The Dining Room in 1861, *a watercolour by James Roberts*.
14. Above   The North Drawing Room in 1861, *a watercolour by James Roberts*.

whole house. On the west side he removed Nash's portico and gave all the first-floor windows arched heads (10). In 1893 the Duke of Edinburgh became Duke of Saxe-Coburg and Gotha and went to live in Germany, retaining the house for his London visits.

There are a few undated photographs of the interior in his time. One shows the Hall with pedimented doorcases and a simple Jacobean-style moulded ceiling, and the walls covered with sporting trophies (17). The room at the southwest corner of the house (now the Morning Room) kept its original coved ceiling but was decorated in a vaguely William Morris way (19). Nash's two separate drawing rooms were linked by a broad opening whose detailing matched the over-mantel glasses and related to the doorcases; the smaller South Room was hung with damask while the larger North Room was devoted to a display of the Duke's trophies (15). However the most remarkable and unexpected interior was the Chapel, fitted up for his Russian wife, and of that fragments still survive (18).

After the Duke of Saxe-Coburg's death in 1900, Clarence House was given to the Duke of Connaught, the third son of Queen Victoria. It was he who had the Dining Room redecorated in an Adam Revival style (94,96) and joined the two Drawing Rooms on the first floor, inserting the present columns (111).

After the death of the Duke of Connaught in 1942 the house was used by the Red Cross and St John's Ambulance for the rest of the Second World War.

In 1947 Clarence House

15. *The Drawing Rooms in the time of the Duke of Edinburgh.*

was chosen as the London house for Princess Elizabeth and the Duke of Edinburgh, and it was restored and modernized for them. How the house was completed and arranged in 1949 is recorded in Christopher Hussey's book *Clarence House*.

After the death of the King in 1952, the new Queen moved to Buckingham Palace and Queen Elizabeth The Queen Mother and Princess Margaret came to Clarence House. Naturally their requirements were rather different from those of Princess Elizabeth and the Duke of Edinburgh (and by then Prince Charles), and these changed yet again after Princess Margaret married in 1960. Thus the plan of the house as it is arranged today is not the same as in 1949, and various other minor structural alterations have been made.

The Hall (59) remains the spine of the house and to the right of it lies the first of the 1870s rooms, the Lancaster Room (73), which since 1949 has been a waiting room for visitors. To the north of that lies the short corridor, now called the Horse Corridor (75), leading from the Hall to the east staircase. Opening off it

16. Above   The Duchess of Kent's Sitting Room in 1861, *a watercolour by James Roberts.*
17. Below   *The Hall in the time of the Duke of Edinburgh.*

on the south side is the Garden Room (80), a drawing room formed out of two rooms added on in 1870, one of which was used by Princess Margaret as her sitting room and the other by the ladies-in-waiting as theirs.

To the left of the Hall is the Morning Room (85), William IV's Breakfast Room and in the late 1940s and early 1950s the Duke of Edinburgh's Room. Queen Elizabeth has linked that by double doors first to the Library (93), formed for Princess Elizabeth out of the original entrance hall, and beyond that to the Dining Room (94, 96) whose decoration dates from early in the Duke of Connaught's time.

Thus Clarence House is a comfortable, spacious house and would meet with the approval of the mid-18th-century Mrs Montagu who, although housing herself much more grandly in Portman Square, wrote that she liked a few large rooms rather than going through a dozen doors before she could sit down.

18. Top *The Russian Chapel created by the Duke of Edinburgh for his Russian wife.*
19. Right *The Morning Room in the time of the Duke of Edinburgh.*

QUEEN ELIZABETH'S APPROACH TO COLLECTING

CLARENCE HOUSE is one of those rare houses in Britain that is now enjoying the most vivid chapter in its history. In part that is due to the range and quality of the pictures, furniture and other objects that Queen Elizabeth has gathered there over the past forty years. But it also depends on the strongly personal atmosphere that she has created: the house comes to life when she is about because of her unconscious gift for blending royal dignity with welcoming informality, the sparkle and darting quality of her conversation, and her expectation of laughter that is as hard to convey in words as her expression is in paint.

Whether the word 'collection' is the right one to use to describe all the things that Queen Elizabeth has assembled at Clarence House is a moot point. It implies a formal purpose, the development of considered aims and the pursuit of certain

20. Left   Holkham Beach *by Edward Seago.*
21. Above   The Sisters: The Daughters of Archdeacon Charles Cavendish-Bentinck *by Sir William Blake Richmond, 1864.*

ideas, but none of that seems to have applied here. Rather it is an accumulation that has grown out of sheer pleasure in pictures and objects, and the enjoyment of the chase after them. Indeed there are surely close parallels between collecting and racing, which King George IV would have recognized, with the satisfaction of a find and purchase being not unlike a win with a home-bred horse.

Gradually the success of the chase has grown into a considerable collection. Arguably the only conscious thread in it has been Queen Elizabeth's concern for family things, both royal and Bowes-Lyon, and the desire to secure pictures and objects that have escaped in the past or might otherwise go wandering now.

22. The Countess of Strathmore *by Mabel Hankey, 1923.*

Perhaps it is because of that essential informality of approach that little has been written about Queen Elizabeth as a collector. So few people realize that she is the first member of the Royal Family to acquire contemporary pictures other than portraits, and to be a patron of artists since Queen Victoria and Prince Albert in the 1840s and 1850s. However, Queen Elizabeth never set out to add a new dimension to the Royal Collection and carry it forward: it was a matter of buying pictures that she enjoyed for her rooms at Buckingham Palace.

Those who have known about this aspect of Queen Elizabeth's life, like the late Lord Clark, have been so loyal and discreet in their memoirs, that it is a case of piecing the story together from scraps of information in a handful of articles and exhibition catalogues, and talking to those who knew the people who helped her. Only Michael Holroyd, in his life of Augustus John, has written fully of the artist's difficulties over his portrait of Queen Elizabeth (81), quoting letters from her to the artist, as we shall see later.

Apart from them, the only other published letter from her about pictures is a particularly moving one written to Edward Seago (1910–74), a Norfolk neighbour and friend, two weeks after the death of the King and quoted in Ron Ranson's *Edward Seago the vintage years* (1992). The Queen had met Mr Seago in 1948 when she sat to him for a portrait for the Royal Air Force College at Cranwell as a pendant to one of the King. The same year she bought her first picture by him, *Yarmouth from Breydon*. Soon after that he became a regular visitor to Sandringham, and he often gave Queen Elizabeth a picture for her birthday, which partly explains why he is more fully represented at Clarence House than any other artist. In her bedroom, for instance, hangs his picture of Holkham beach, a favourite place to go from Sandringham (20).

The Queen and Princess Margaret drove over from Sandringham to see Edward Seago the day before the King died, and in her letter Her Majesty wrote:

I have been longing to write and tell you what real pleasure your lovely pictures gave the King ... I got back to Sandringham rather late, and as I always did, rushed straight to the King's room to say that I was back and to see how he was. I found him so well, so gay and so interested in our lovely cruise on the river; and then I told him that you had sent the pictures back in my car and we went straight to the Hall where they had been set out. He was enchanted with them all, and we spent a very happy time looking at them together.

We had such a truly gay dinner, with the King like his old self, and more picture looking after dinner ...

That infectious pleasure in pictures and objects goes back to Queen Elizabeth's childhood, to her family's houses, of which more will be said in the next section, and the influences of her mother, her mother's younger unmarried sister, and her maternal grandmother. In 1881 her father, then Lord Glamis and later 14th Earl of Strathmore, had married her mother, Nina Cecilia Cavendish-Bentinck, the eldest

23. Lady Elizabeth Bowes-Lyon *by Mabel Hankey, about 1908.*

daughter of Archdeacon Charles William Frederick Cavendish-Bentinck, a grandson of the 3rd Duke of Portland, and his second wife, Caroline Louisa Burnaby.

Queen Elizabeth's parents lived mainly at St Paul's Walden Bury in Hertfordshire. Queen Elizabeth is the last but one of a spread-out family of ten children. Since her next older brother was seven years older and her next older sister ten years older, she and her younger brother, David, were much the youngest in the nursery. There their mother (22) played an active role in their formal as well as their informal education: teaching them to read and write, and going on drives into Hitchin, the town near St Paul's, to take note of what they saw. Lady Strathmore pointed out to her daughter that a certain 18th-century brick house was a beautiful house while a later Regency or Victorian white house was an ugly one. That was a lesson that has never been forgotten, and encouraged Queen Elizabeth to teach her grandchildren to use their eyes.

It was about that time the first portrait of Queen Elizabeth (23) was painted by Mabel Hankey, an artist who appears to have been a favourite of Lady Strathmore, and it may have been shown at the Royal Academy in 1907. Mabel Hankey, who exhibited between 1889 and 1914 and died in 1943, painted three other pictures of Queen Elizabeth, a miniature at the age of five, another at the age of seventeen and a final one in a jewelled frame that was Lady Strathmore's wedding present to the Duke of York. Her portrait of Lady Strathmore was painted in 1923 (22).

24. Left   Madonna and Child *by the Master of the Castello Nativity, about 1460.*
25. Below   Children Offering Flowers to Venus; The Personification of Music; The Personification of Poetry *by Riccardo Meacci (born 1856).*

An early memory of the future Queen's response to pictures and objects is of her going to the house of the Minister at Glamis, Mr Stinton, during the course of the family's annual holiday. Many years ago he recorded that Lady Elizabeth:

... was particularly fond of coming up to see my collection of family relics and curios, and showed a wonderful knowledge of these things for so little a child. I have a note from her, written at a very early age, in which she asks if she and her governess might come up and see my 'objays d'art'. She was particularly fascinated by my portrait of Prince Charles Edward Stuart.

That curiosity is surely important to understanding how Queen Elizabeth became a collector in the late 1930s, and gives particular point to the portrait of the Old Pretender and his sister by Largillière at the foot of the stairs at Clarence House (71).

26. *One of a pair of antique angels bought by Queen Elizabeth when aged about eight.*

Queen Elizabeth's grandmother, Mrs Cavendish-Bentinck, married as her second husband Henry Warren Scott of Ancrum, and so comes into living memory as Mrs Scott. In 1882 Mrs Scott, by then a widow again, went to live in Florence at Villa Capponi, where she designed the garden. She also had a villa at Bordighera and an apartment in Rome as well as Forbes House at Ham, near Richmond. The impression her houses and gardens created can still be gathered from the memories of Lady Ottoline Morrell, the daughter of her first husband's younger brother and the sister of the 6th Duke of Portland. Of Forbes House Lady Ottoline wrote: 'The old house was filled with Italian furniture and pictures, and the perfume of tiger-lilies, and it was to me a haven of joy.' Later, memories of the garden at Villa Capponi inspired Lady Ottoline's famous garden at Garsington Manor, near Oxford.

In her authorized book about the Duchess of York published in 1928, Lady Cynthia Asquith wrote an account of Villa Capponi that has the ring of

27. A bedhead painted for Queen Elizabeth by Riccardo Meacci in 1923.

personal reminiscence about it that could have come from the Duchess or her brother, David:

Inside everything was in perfect harmony with the surroundings, and one can imagine how impressive to a child must have been the great room with an organ at one end, a fireplace in the centre and dark panelled walls – a stately solemn room, yet full of comfort and brightness. Lovely furniture, flowers, books, beauty everywhere. And the little chapel with its few exquisite pictures, and walls covered with red damask.

Of Mrs Scott's earlier Italianate taste there is one evocative picture at Clarence House: the picture of her three daughters painted in 1864 by Sir William Blake Richmond that hangs in the Drawing Room (21).

It was Mrs Scott and even more her younger daughter, Violet, who lived with her, who opened her granddaughter's eyes to Italian Renaissance and more particularly Florentine painting in the course of visits to Italy before 1914. Queen Elizabeth still talks of being taken by her aunt to look at pictures, one at a time, in the Uffizi Gallery and Pitti Palace – with a thimble full of vermouth afterwards at Doneys. Thus Botticelli's *Primavera* is still vivid in her mind's eye.

28. The Madonna and Child with St John *by Raffaelino del Garbo (1479?–1527?)*.

Today the most visible signs of Queen Elizabeth's early Florentine experience at Clarence House are the *Madonna and Child* by the Master of the Castello Nativity (about 1460) (24), which belonged to Mrs Scott and now hangs in the Garden Room, and the *Madonna and Child* (about 1450) now ascribed to Zanobi Strozzi or the Master of the Buckingham Palace Madonna, which hangs in her Sitting Room (118). The importance of early religious painting, however, only becomes apparent in Queen Elizabeth's Bedroom with its tondo of *The Madonna and Child with St John* by Raffaelino del Garbo (1479?–1527?) (28), which was also inherited from Mrs Scott and hangs over the chimneypiece, close to the little pictures by Meacci.

When Queen Elizabeth married the Duke of York in 1923, a bed was painted for her in the Renaissance style by Riccardo Meacci (27) (who was born in 1856 and worked mainly in Siena), and carved by a colleague of his. Meacci must have been known to Mrs Scott and her daughters, because he is mentioned in a catalogue which survives of an exhibition of the Royal Amateur Art Society held from 8 to 11 March 1906 at 1 Belgrave Square in aid of charities.

Lady Strathmore lent six pictures, whose subjects are not given, but the list of fellow lenders and pictures corresponds very closely to the otherwise mysterious little pictures in a Florentine Renaissance Revival style on the chimneypiece in Queen Elizabeth's Bedroom. She has known the pictures all her life. They are of *Saint Martin Dividing His Cloak* and three pictures in one frame of *Children Offering Flowers to Venus*; *The Personification of Music* and *The Personification of Poetry* by Meacci (25). With them there is another by Sandrino Catani of *The Triumphal Entry of a Knight* that is signed and dated 'Firenze 1910'. There are more pictures in this vein at Royal Lodge as well as in the Royal Collection.

On the head posts of the bed stand two angels with pointed wings and real robes (26). They seem to be so much part of the design that it is a surprise to discover that they are additions made by Queen Elizabeth and, in fact, were her first purchases, made when she was about eight years old. She saw them in Bordighera, when staying with her grandmother, and remembers buying them – for three lire – after bargaining.

In the early years of her marriage to the Duke of York, Queen Elizabeth was concentrating on setting up home rather than collecting in a formal sense, and no purchases of pictures other than portraits from that period stand out at Clarence House. Their first house was White Lodge in Richmond Park, the house that is now occupied by the Royal Ballet. Since it had been her childhood home, Queen Mary was delighted to see them take it on and took great trouble to prepare it for them. However it was too large and inconvenient as well as too far from central London for the Duke and Duchess of York's public life, and they soon began to look for another house. Finally in 1927 they took 145 Piccadilly, of which there are illustrations in Lady Cynthia Asquith's book, *The Duchess of York* (1928). They furnished it with mainly late-18th-century furniture, but, like many of the rooms of that time, they now seem rather sparse. In 1931 King George V offered them the Royal Lodge in Windsor Great Park, which called for a great deal of

29. & 30. The Duke and Duchess of York *by Philip de Laszlo, 1931*.

work on the house, including the restoration of the Gothic dining room formed by Wyatville for King George IV. They also began to make an informal woodland garden.

The late 1920s and early 1930s, it must be remembered, were years of economic depression, with a particularly serious crisis in 1931, when the Civil List was cut. The Duke of York decided that he must give up his horses and hunting, and Nancy Lancaster recalls in her recent memoirs how he did not take a house in the Pytchley country for the season of 1931–2 and never returned. The Duke wrote to her husband, Ronald Tree: 'It had come as a great shock to me that with the economy cuts I have had to make my hunting should have been one of the things I must do without ... And I must sell my horses too. This is the worst part of it all and the parting with them will be terrible.'

It was only in 1937 after King George VI succeeded his brother that the Queen started to make serious purchases of works of art. The first were objects that related to the history of the Royal Family, which had been Queen Mary's main interest. This has continued to be important to Queen Elizabeth, with some of her acquisitions being made for the Royal Collection and now hung either in the royal palaces or at Clarence House. A few are worth mentioning here, because it is not generally realized what Queen Elizabeth has added to the Royal

31. & 32. *Busts of Charles I and William III attributed to Francis Bird (1667–1731), now in the State Rooms at Windsor Castle.*

Collection. Sculpture, for instance, was hardly a popular field at the time. In 1937 Queen Elizabeth bought for the Royal Collection busts of Charles I and William III that appeared at Christie's. They have been attributed to Francis Bird (1667–1731), and that of Charles I being after a cast of the Bernini bust lost in the fire at Whitehall Palace in 1698 (31, 32). The same year she bought a cabinet inlaid with ebony, tortoiseshell and ivory and enclosing ivory carvings representing the *Apotheosis of James II* done by Matthieu van Beveren, an Antwerp sculptor, about 1685 (33, 34). That was drawn to her attention by Lord Gerald Wellesley, the architect and connoisseur who served as Surveyor of the King's Works of Art from 1936 to 1944 and became 7th Duke of Wellington. In 1948 it was at her suggestion that an equestrian statuette of Charles I after Hubert Le Sueur (working *c.*1610–51) was acquired; it is a reduced version of his statue of the King at the top of Whitehall, and it appears to have been in Charles I's Cabinet at Whitehall in 1639 (36). Three years later she acquired the haunting portrait of *Charles I at his Trial* by Edward Bower (recorded 1629–died 1667), which is one of at least four known versions (35).

As far as recent portraits are concerned it is apparent that Queen Elizabeth has always preferred the immediacy of sketches to highly finished formal portraits, of which she probably found more than enough around her. This lighter aspect of portraiture is important to the mood of Clarence House today, being

33. & 34. *A cabinet with ivory panels representing the* Apotheosis of James II *by Matthieu van Beveren, about 1685, now in the Private Apartments at Windsor Castle.*

complementary to her taste in 20th-century pictures. Most of the portraits of the King and herself are either studies or sketches or unfinished (62,63,81,82,97, 109,110,122,123). That also applies to the two portraits of King George V (90,109) and the principal pictures of Queen Victoria by David Wilkie and Edwin Landseer (116,113); and King George IV is represented in a fine drawing by Thomas Lawrence (117).

Queen Elizabeth has always been a responsive sitter, as several artists and Cecil Beaton have recorded, and a very patient one, accepting that a portrait can be a struggle for the painter as well as a disappointment for the sitter. She has been as generous as possible with her time and in meeting the requests of those who have wished to paint her. The result at Clarence House is a remarkable series that will surely seem increasingly good as the years pass and 20th-century traditional painting becomes more appreciated: from J. S. Sargent and Savely Sorine, it goes on to de Laszlo, with Gerald Kelly, Augustus John, James Gunn and Graham Sutherland all on view (86,106,29,122,81,82,97), and others like John Bratby providing

35. Charles I at his Trial *by Edward Bower.*

a shock when they emerge from a stack.

As well as buying historical objects for the Royal Collection, the Queen also bought some furniture to introduce a fresh, less formidable note into the splendid but ungiving palace rooms. In 1938, for instance, she bought the very colourful scarlet lacquer and silver gesso cabinet-on-stand that is now in the Drawing Room at Clarence House (115). Surprisingly the Royal Collection is not rich in elegant English 18th-century furniture of any phase, with George III and Queen Charlotte only being represented by the finest carved pieces in the manner of Vile and Cobb. The simpler, pretty furniture that Queen Charlotte must have had in her private rooms at Windsor has virtually all gone, and Queen Elizabeth found a real lack of furniture dating from the second half of the 18th century, particularly chairs, that she had grown up with and liked to live with.

Over the years she has bought interesting furniture for her rooms (37,39), but without it taking on that set look that tends to be so marked in the more formal collections of English furniture concentrating on walnut and carved mahogany built up between 1910 and 1960. Queen Elizabeth has preferred lighter forms associated with the Adam period, with parcel gilded or gilded decoration, and the less monumental Regency furniture that became fashionable in the 1920s and 1930s (39).

The 1940s and 1950s were a good time to buy because of the frequent country house sales, and a number of those houses are now represented at Clarence House. There is a range of pieces bought at the Wentworth Woodhouse sale in 1948. From Ditchley Park, Oxfordshire, came a fine mirror with a mask of Diana originally made for one of the principal rooms on the west side of the house that were fitted up about 1740 by Henry Flitcroft — originally sold from Ditchley (37) in 1932 and acquired, along with a pair of torchères that are now at Windsor Castle, in 1945. And, most spectacular of all, is the set of late-18th-century drawing-room furniture from Preston Hall, Midlothian (39). Queen Elizabeth also bought furniture at the 1946 sale of Woolmers Park, in Hertfordshire, a house her father had bought after he had made over St Paul's Walden Bury to his youngest son and which was sold following his death. However some of her best purchases, like the pair of commodes (79) in the Garden Room, have no old provenance.

36. *An equestrian statuette of Charles I after Hubert Le Sueur (working c.1610–51). It was bought for the Royal Collection at Queen Elizabeth's suggestion in 1948.*

Queen Elizabeth has always enjoyed hunting for objects and making finds, and this must have been a bond with her mother-in-law, Queen Mary, for whom antique shops had two great advantages over shooting: there was no close season and they could be sought anywhere. Most weeks when in London Queen Elizabeth would go with Queen Mary to shops, not just in New Oxford Street and Bond Street but in the East End as well. But if on her own Queen Elizabeth bought something that Queen Mary felt more suited to Marlborough House, off it would disappear. This happened with the portrait of George III when Prince of Wales, which did not come back until after Queen Mary's death (65).

Queen Mary loved objects, and particularly small ones with royal associations, but she was not interested in pictures as such. Here Queen Elizabeth was fortunate to know both Sir Jasper Ridley and Sir Kenneth Clark. Since Sir Kenneth is better known as a collector and patron of modern artists and was both Surveyor

37. *A glass from Ditchley Park, Oxfordshire, about 1740.*

of the King's Pictures and Director of the National Gallery, it would be reasonable to presume that his influence was the more important. In fact, it was probably Sir Jasper's which was more significant. Sir Jasper had been a friend of Queen Elizabeth before her marriage. He was the second son of Sir Matthew Ridley, 5th baronet and later 1st Viscount Ridley; he was born in 1887, and in 1911 he married Countess Natalie Benckendorff. A barrister by training, Sir Jasper became a banker and was chairman of Coutts Bank.

Sir Jasper began to buy contemporary pictures as early as 1909–10 and kept a careful record of his purchases from 1913. This means it is possible to see how someone with an eye, imagination and confidence could gradually build up a collection spending less than £200 a year (and in at least half the years less than £100) and yet have fun. He was interested in both British and French painting, happily buying drawings, watercolours and prints when he could not afford paintings, and also in sculpture. His first important purchase of a contemporary picture was Mark Gertler's *Creation of Eve* in 1915. By 1926 he was sufficiently established as a collector of contemporary pictures to become a member of the Committee of the Contemporary Art Society; later in 1942–3 he served as its Honorary Treasurer and then as its Honorary Secretary. Sir Jasper was chairman of the Trustees of the Tate Gallery and a Trustee of both the National Gallery and the British Museum.

From the point of view of Queen Elizabeth's pictures, it is interesting to know which artists they both bought. Ethel Walker, for instance, occurs in Sir Jasper's accounts in 1927 when he bought a watercolour of the Yorkshire coast. He bought an early Sickert drawing of Mornington Crescent in 1935 and John Piper's *Approach to Fonthill* in 1940, followed by a watercolour of *Welsh Mountains* in 1941 for £12. That year he bought a pair of Sickert etchings including one of *Ennui*. In 1942 he bought John Piper's *Llanthony Abbey* and in 1944 a Matthew Smith *Southern French*

Landscape for what was a large price for him of £125. But Sir Jasper went much further, buying a Stanley Spencer oil in 1936, paintings and water-colours by John Minton and Keith Vaughan, a *Shelter Study* and later small bronzes by Henry Moore and a nude by Ruskin Spear, a landscape by J.B. Yeats and a water-colour by Graham Suther-land. While he was collecting on a more modest scale than Sir Kenneth, clearly he kept a close eye on what was to be seen in West End galleries in a way that is now hardly ever fun for collectors of modest means.

38. *The Duke of York, Lady Elizabeth Bowes-Lyon and Arthur Penn at Glamis Castle in 1921. A snapshot in Sir Arthur Penn's game book, pasted in with photographs taken at Balmoral in September 1937.*

Although made a KCVO, Sir Jasper was never a member of the Queen's House-hold, but he remained a devoted and helpful friend until he died in 1951.

Both Sir Jasper and Sir Kenneth would tell the Queen of pictures they had seen on their rounds of galleries and exhibitions which they thought might appeal to her, and then either she would visit the gallery or the pictures would be sent round for her to see. The process was so informal and direct that there are prob-ably no letters to cast light on it, although dealers' names are recorded in the card index. And, as will be seen with John Piper's commission to paint Windsor Castle, both men were involved.

While their interests were in pictures, there was a third, more important figure drawn to furniture, porcelain and clocks. He was Sir Arthur Penn, again a friend of Queen Elizabeth since before her marriage and with a complementary sense of humour (38), and he also happened to be an old friend of Sir Jasper Ridley. Sir Arthur served Queen Elizabeth as Acting Private Secretary from 1940 to 1946 and then as her Treasurer until his death on the day before he was due to retire at the end of 1960. Born in 1886, he was the grandson of John Penn, a brilliant and

39. One of the set of chairs with verre eglomisé decoration, from Preston Hall, Midlothian, about 1790.

successful marine engineer, who, among other ships, fitted the engine to HMS *Warrior*. After Cambridge he trained as a barrister, like Sir Jasper, and then he went into the City, becoming chairman of the bill brokers King & Shaxson. During the First World War Sir Arthur served in the Grenadier Guards and was wounded. In 1937 he became a member of the King's Household as a Groom in Waiting and in 1940 an Extra Equerry. At the outbreak of the Second World War he rejoined the Grenadiers and from 1941 to 1945 served as Regimental Adjutant, being responsible for the problems of the wounded and of the families of those killed. Thus for the duration of the War he had two offices, one at Wellington Barracks and a second at Buckingham Palace, where he served the Queen.

It was while he was at Cambridge that he began to buy objects and from 1910 he carefully recorded all his purchases. Having a very good eye he loved browsing in sale rooms and in antique shops, and he had a gift for finding skilled craftsmen and enjoyed the processes of design and restoration, later playing a leading role in the extension of Birkhall for Queen Elizabeth and the restoration of the Castle of Mey. It was he who encouraged the Queen to share his pleasure in mirrors, chinoiserie, clocks and early Chelsea, all fields now strongly represented at Clarence House.

Sadly the notes Sir Arthur sent about objects that he had seen and thought might appeal to her, together with her reactions, have disappeared. They must have had a great deal of fun as can be gathered from Queen Elizabeth's response to one sale catalogue: 'they usually say a thousand pounds for something hideous, which goes for a hundred, and a hundred pounds for something lovely that goes for a thousand.' Clearly Sir Arthur had a real feeling for what she liked. That can be gathered in a brief extract from Queen Elizabeth's letter of thanks for his

34

40. Chepstow Castle *by Philip Wilson Steer, 1906.*

birthday present in 1944, which also reveals her own seeing eye for even modest objects: 'I am simply enchanted with the *lovely* teapot and plates. Thank you a thousand times for something so delicious. Hardly any one likes Whieldon pottery and I love seeing their faces of disgust when they see the glutinous brown, green, yellow so nicely blended to *my* mind.'

The card index of pictures still gives a sense of rapidly growing confidence, curiosity and delight in the chase, with the particular excitement of buying the first pictures by living artists in 1938: Wilson Steer's *Chepstow Castle* (40) and one of Augustus John's portraits of G. B. Shaw called *When Homer Nods* (91). These artists were the established figures of the older generation, with Steer and Sickert representing the British interest in Impressionism, rather than those who were younger and still up and coming, but the latter's turn was to come.

The cards also give a remarkable sense of the sustaining qualities of wartime purchases when the royal palaces were largely stripped and works of art at

41. October Morning *by Ethel Walker, 1938.*

Buckingham Palace were replaced by buckets and baths to catch the leaks through the damaged roof (which the Queen asked Cecil Beaton to photograph, a series, alas, not recorded in the Royal Archives). The Queen felt the need for visual and spiritual refreshment and saw it as an act of faith and defiance to Hitler to carry on encouraging artists and making purchases.

When it was clear that war was inevitable, Sir Kenneth's first concern was to see that the pictures were removed from the National Gallery and the Royal Collection to places of safety. However even before the Gallery closed on 23 August 1939, he was thinking about a scheme for war artists that would combine a patriotic purpose with safeguarding certain talented people. Soon he also began to think about a new role for the National Gallery, which grew out of Myra Hess's suggestion made in late September 1939, that concerts should be held in the empty Gallery, and out of Lillian Browse's suggestion that exhibitions of British

36

painting should be held there. As a result more than twenty exhibitions were put on at the National Gallery, quite apart from the constantly changing display of the work of the war artists that started in July 1940, and there are many signs of the Queen's interest in them. She lent her Ethel Walker *October Morning* (41) and her Augustus John *When Homer Nods* (91) to the first and most ambitious exhibition organized by Lillian Browse as *British Painting Since Whistler*.

A second event, planned for September 1940, had to be cancelled because the increase in bombing meant that it was no longer safe to use the main floor of the Gallery. Consequently exhibitions had to be more limited in scope. However the preface to the 1941 *Whistler and Early-20th-Century Oils* and *Six Water Colour Painters of Today* gives an idea of the mood: 'It is to be hoped that the present small exhibitions may also be primarily regarded as a refreshment for the mind and an exercise for the spirit at a time when the very defence of the activities of the mind and of the spirit give few opportunities for their enjoyment . . .'

That seems to provide the key to the Queen's acquisitions in those years.

Queen Elizabeth had the idea of having a series of paintings of Windsor Castle, because, as she says, she did not know whether or not it would be bombed. So when in August 1941, she went to the first 'Recording Britain' exhibition at the National Gallery, Sir Kenneth suggested that she should commission John Piper. Not only did that prove to be her most important commission but also it was a crucial one for Piper (74).

The 1941 exhibitions were followed by a Sickert exhibition to which the Queen lent her *Ennui*. On several occasions she attended concerts at the Gallery, and when in March 1942, she slipped into one of them, she was photographed sharing her programme with her neighbour.

On 18 May 1945, nine days after the end of the war in Europe, the King and Queen visited the National Gallery to welcome back the first fifty pictures.

Thus what the King and Queen were doing was to give active support to a movement that was not only psychologically important at the time but which after the war was to bear such a range of practical new fruit that we now take for granted. The idea of public responsibility and support for the Arts, the Arts Council, public support for the Tate Gallery's purchase fund, all grew out of what Sir Kenneth Clark and his colleagues were up to in the WAAC (War Artists Advisory Committee) and at the National Gallery. Similarly the idea of the 'Recording Britain' project related to the establishment in 1941 of the National Buildings Record to collect photographs of historic buildings that might be destroyed, a scheme that eventually grew into the idea of listing historic buildings and protecting them by law.

The Windsor commission unites two threads: the feeling that the castle might be destroyed and the growing appreciation of the English romantic tradition and of the English achievement in architecture and painting that was fostered by John Betjeman and his circle, and in the books published by Batsfords and in Collins' *Britain in Pictures* series. Piper's Windsor drawings, delivered in 1942 and 1944, bring to mind his other great series that grew out of them in 1942–3, that of Renishaw Hall, in Derbyshire, for Sir Osbert Sitwell to use as illustrations in his autobiography *Left Hand, Right Hand.*

When thinking about the Queen's 20th-century purchases and commissions, this combination of patriotism and romanticism comes very much to mind, and it is surely very remarkable to sense that, not in a museum or a historic monument, but in the private house of someone who was playing a leading role in the life of the country over fifty years ago. It is a private aspect of the public face of Her Majesty that was so inspiring at the time and that was so powerfully recalled to mind in her appearances during the celebrations in 1995 commemorating the end of the Second World War and the response that she evoked once again.

At the end of the war Buckingham Palace was gradually put into order, but it was only after 1947 that the Queen was able to take her pictures out of store and arrange them in her private rooms. The card index provides a few clues about what she did, but regrettably there appear to be no photographs of the rooms. In the Tea Room adjoining her Sitting Room the pictures generally included the Stevens, Steer, Sickerts, Nash, Monet and one of the Johns, although there were frequent changes to fill gaps when pictures went away on loan to exhibitions.

With the departure of Sir Kenneth from the Surveyorship of the King's Pictures in 1944 and the death of Sir Jasper in 1951, but with the continuation of Sir Arthur for another ten years until his death at the end of 1960, it was natural that there should have been a change of emphasis in Queen Elizabeth's acquisitions. That is particularly apparent in her collecting of Chelsea porcelain (126–9) of the Red Anchor period (1752–6). Although she had acquired her first pieces of Chelsea, a pair of dishes modelled as sunflowers, in 1937, the years 1945–51 were her most active ones in that direction, and she continued to add to her collection during the 1950s. She has concentrated on pieces originally intended for the table rather than figures, and essentially informal in character: an equivalent of the kind of gardening that she and The King enjoyed at Royal Lodge.

It was because of her known enthusiasm for Chelsea that in 1947 Queen Elizabeth was presented by James Oakes with part of the most spectacular and historically most interesting service ever made at Chelsea. She decided that the gift should become part of the Royal Collection. The service was ordered in 1762 by George III and Queen Charlotte for the Queen's brother, Duke Adolphus Frederick of Mecklenburg-Strelitz. Although of splendid quality with superb painting, it lacks the charm of Red Anchor pieces and it is interesting that Queen Elizabeth has bought no examples of that later, richer Chelsea for herself.

Among more recent acquisitions the one group that calls out for mention is that of the Australian pictures that have given their name to the corridor over the Horse Corridor that leads from the Upper Corridor to the east staircase. Queen Elizabeth first went to Australia in 1927 with the Duke of York and she went again in 1971. Her feeling for that vast con-tinent is expressed in Sydney Nolan's *Green Swamp*,

42. Still Life with Matisse *by Duncan Grant, 1947.*

Kenneth Jack's *Storm Approaching Marree* (43), which was painted in 1965, and Russell Drysdale's *Home Leave* of 1943 (44).

The collection at Clarence House, however, does not consist solely of pictures, furniture and Chelsea, because Queen Elizabeth has a love of small, exquisite objects – snuff boxes, oriental snuff bottles, Fabergé (103, 104,), and Battersea and Chelsea toys. Some cabinets are now almost bursting.

After the death of Sir Arthur at the end of 1960, Queen Elizabeth was helped in her acquisitions by Lord Adam Gordon, who had been her Comptroller since 1953. As with Sir Jasper and Sir Arthur there were long-standing family friend-ships, because his mother, Mrs Douglas Gordon, was a friend of Lady Elphinstone, one of Queen Elizabeth's elder sisters, and Queen Elizabeth had been one of her bridesmaids at her wedding. Lord Adam was a keen collector as well as a pas-sionate gardener, and not only did he go to look at pictures and objects that inter-ested Queen Elizabeth, but he would also tell her of things that he had seen on his rounds. In the early 1960s a considerable number of acquisitions were made,

43. Storm Approaching Marree *by Kenneth Jack*, *1965*.

among them the Bassano in the Garden Room, the Largillière in the Hall (71) and the Wilkie drawings for the picture of Princess Victoria in the Drawing Room. Unfortunately prices were rising and the chase was becoming less enjoyable and after 1967 there were few significant purchases. However even after Lord Adam gave up being Comptroller in 1973, he used to tell Queen Elizabeth of things that he had seen and thought might appeal to her.

The great surprise at Clarence House is the plate (47,48,52,54,94–6,130–41), which can also be regarded as the senior element in the collection in that the first pieces were wedding presents in 1923 (130). Acquisitions and presentations have been made in every decade since then. As with the pictures and furniture, it is not really a formal collection, nor is it concerned with the development of styles or particular makers: it is very much for use in the Dining Room. The history of pieces, however, has been frequently taken into account, and been the determining factor. Many pieces have a royal or Bowes or Bowes-Lyon history. There are also a number of recent pieces like a gold box given to her by the Fishmongers'

44. Home Leave *by Russell Drysdale, 1943.*

Company, which opens to reveal a silver fish, and the Leslie Durbin silver-gilt trochus shells given to Queen Elizabeth in 1960 by the Anglo-American Corporation after she opened the Kariba Dam (5). They are used frequently and with pleasure.

In thinking about the range of pictures and objects in the house, fascinating cross threads emerge between objects in different materials. There are comparisons to be drawn between the silver-gilt salad dishes made by Samuel Wakelin (137) and the Chelsea Red Anchor plates (126–8) modelled after the leaves and flowers (127,129). There is also a range of objects that reflect Queen Elizabeth's enthusiasm for chinoiserie: the pair of clocks in the Hall and Drawing Room (60,115) can be compared with the pair of mid-18th-century painted glasses in gilded frames in the Garden Room (79) and a set of three Rococo silver-gilt tea caddies by William Cripps (139) and the pair of Rococo Revival candlesticks made by Edward Farrell in 1821 (141). For anyone who enjoys jigsaws, Clarence House provides a visual and historical field day.

THE BOWES-LYON THREAD
AT CLARENCE HOUSE

A SENSE OF family, present and past, is one of the strongest themes at Clarence House and in what Queen Elizabeth has acquired over the past sixty years. Alongside royal pictures and objects are many that relate to Queen Elizabeth's own family, the Bowes-Lyons. But since their history is both less familiar and also complicated, it may be helpful to readers to let the Bowes, Lyon and Bowes-Lyon objects and the houses from which they come tell their own story.

Queen Elizabeth is invariably thought of as Scottish but, in fact, the house where she spent most of her childhood was in England, St Paul's Walden Bury in Hertfordshire, which had come to her family by marriage in 1767 (45). It is hard

45. *St Paul's Walden Bury, Hertfordshire, the North Front.*

42

46. *Glamis Castle, Forfarshire, a watercolour by Paul Sandby, about 1750. It was given to Queen Elizabeth by Her Household on her 70th birthday.*

to think of an 18th-century place that could be more stimulating to a child with a visual bent. The house now appears as an understated mid-18th-century building and it is set in a slightly earlier formal garden of the rarest type in England, with allées and glades of pleached trees and trim hedges and accents of contemporary sculpture, that was laid out in the 1720s or 1730s. The principal rooms have elegant decoration of the 1760s, and old photographs show them hung with Italian Renaissance pictures. That synthesis has always meant a great deal to Queen Elizabeth.

How it came about is not entirely clear. The garden and the centre of the house are the work of Edward Gilbert. His only daughter, Mary, married George Bowes of Streatlam and Gibside in Co. Durham as his second wife in 1743. The date on the rainwater hoppers on the wings is 1767, which is the year George Bowes's only daughter, Mary Eleanor, married the 9th Earl of Strathmore. So it is not clear whether Mrs George Bowes added on the wings after the death of her husband in 1760 or whether they should be associated with the early days of the Strathmore marriage. Lady Strathmore, as we will see, had a tragic life partly through her own lack of judgement, and she was succeeded at St Paul's by her grandson, the son of the 11th Earl, who died before his father. It then went to her grandson's

43

47. *A silver dish with the arms and monogram with coronet of the 3rd Earl of Strathmore, 1684.*

widow, who lived until 1881. She restored the place to the main line of the family by giving it to her great-nephew, Lord Glamis, Queen Elizabeth's father, who became 14th Earl of Strathmore in 1904.

It was the return of St Paul's to the main line of the family and to Lord Glamis (as he then was), that explains why Queen Elizabeth's parents spent most of the year there. Glamis Castle in Forfar, which only came with the Earldom, was the place the family went to in late summer and early autumn (46).

It is hard to think of a greater contrast in Britain between the two places: the calm, sensible, red brick and cheerful domestic scale of St Paul's and the pinky-grey stone and dramatic silhouette of Glamis. The way the castle builds up from its swept-back wings with round towers to the great central tower, bristling with bartizans, steep conical roofs and columnar chimneys, is thrilling.

Moreover Glamis is a place of legend and romance, violence and tragedy, through its associations with King Malcolm who died there of his wounds in 1034; King Duncan, who was murdered there in 1040 by Macbeth; the wife of the 5th Lord Glamis, who was burnt for witchcraft; and Mary Queen of Scots, who visited the 7th Lord Glamis.

The late-17th- and early-18th-century history is particularly complicated. In 1677 the 3rd Earl of Kinghorne was created Earl of Strathmore and Kinghorne (but he and his successors have always kept to the traditional numbering, although *The Complete Peerage* corrects that). He was the great restorer of Glamis and was largely responsible for giving it its present appearance. His father had incurred heavy debts first through supporting the Covenanters and then Charles I; and after he died in 1646, the three-year-old boy was badly treated by his

48. *A late-17th-century silver coffee pot and stand, probably Chinese, inscribed 'Lady Lizh Stanhope, Countess of Strathmore'.*

49. *Streatlam Castle, Co. Durham, in 1915 (now demolished).*

stepfather. When he finally came into control of his estates, the 3rd Earl was faced by heavy debts and buildings in poor condition. However he pulled everything round, and it was he who imposed a degree of symmetry on the old castle and gave it its romantic silhouette.

The 3rd Earl also acquired a quantity of plate including the oval silver rose-water dish of 1684, which Queen Elizabeth bought in 1948 (47). The year 1684 was a key year for Lord Strathmore as far as silver was concerned, because, according to his *Book of Records*, he bought £3,000 Scots worth of new and old plate from James Cockburn of Edinburgh. Cockburn also agreed to remove the existing armorials and engrave the Strathmore arms in their place, as happened on the Strathmore salver by Alexander Scott of 1670, now in the Royal Museum of Scotland.

Both the 3rd Earl, who died in 1695, and his son, John, are represented by portraits at Clarence House. The latter, who was born in 1663, married Lady Elizabeth Stanhope, daughter of the Earl of Chesterfield, in 1691, an event perhaps marked by Lord Glamis's portrait which is dated that year. His wife is represented by a Chinese silver coffee pot and stand, a rare and puzzling object (48). Chinoiserie decoration appeared on English silver in the 1680s, but usually etched on to English forms, whereas the coffee pot is an oriental version of an

46

English shape and is heavier than contemporary English plate. It seems to be part of a small number of pieces of oriental silver without assay marks recorded in England and difficult to date more closely than the late 17th or early 18th century. The coffee pot was in the sale of Strathmore silver at Christie's in 1948 and, given Queen Elizabeth's enthusiasm for chinoiserie, not surprisingly she did not let it go.

The 4th Earl was a quiet opponent of both the Revolution and the Union. Suspected of Jacobite sympathies, he only just managed to avoid arrest and trial for high treason, dying aged only 49 in 1712.

Since his two elder sons had died before him, he was succeeded by his third son and then in turn by his remaining three sons: John, who came out for the Pretender and was killed at the Battle of Sheriffmuir in 1715; Charles, who entertained the Pretender at Glamis and died at the age of only 28 after

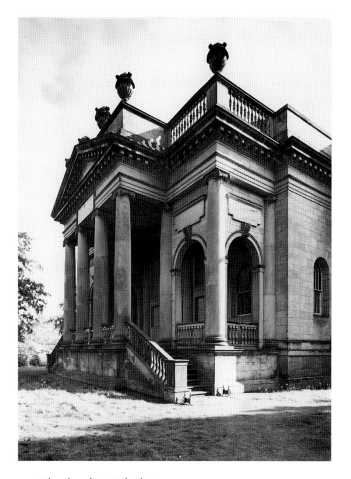

50. *The chapel at Gibside in 1952.*

being stabbed in a brawl in Forfar; James, who died at the age of 32 in 1735; and finally Thomas, the 8th Earl, who died at the age of 48 in 1753. However the last had a son, John, the 9th Earl, who married Mary Eleanor Bowes.

It was probably in the 8th Earl's time that Paul Sandby visited Glamis and did the watercolour that Her Majesty's Household presented to her on her 70th birthday (46). It shows the castle framed by allées of trees and the forecourt still enclosed by the wall and gates built by the 3rd Earl. Paul Sandby had followed his elder brother into army service and in 1747 was appointed official draughtsman to the Military Survey in Scotland, set up after the crushing of the 1745 rebellion to work on maps of the Highlands. He remained in Scotland for about five years. The drawing was probably used for the view of Glamis in Watts's *Seats* published in 1779.

Lady Bowes,
Wife of Sir Thomas Bowes

51. *An early-17th-century portrait of Lady Bowes. It is the earliest portrait at Clarence House.*

In addition to St Paul's and Glamis, Queen Elizabeth's parents also had Streatlam Castle, in Co. Durham, a handsome north country Baroque house that had been the principal Bowes seat since the second quarter of the 14th century, when it had been acquired by marriage (49). That too had come back to the main line in 1885. The family went there for a two-week visit every year in the years before the First World War. However in 1922 Lord Strathmore decided to sell it and that was followed by a disastrous dispersal of the contents. Five years later the fabric was stripped, and what remained was finally blown up in 1959.

Gibside had come back to the Strathmores at the same time as Streatlam, but Queen Elizabeth's parents never lived in the Jacobean house there. However the landscape with its monuments, chapel and mausoleum was maintained, and the family used to drive over from Streatlam.

The chapel (50) was given to the National Trust by the 16th Earl of Strathmore in 1965, and in 1993 the Trust bought 400 acres including the ruins of the hall, the orangery and the Column of Liberty.

The combination of places of such different characters and histories

52. *The silver-gilt sideboard dish and ewer by David Willaume, 1718. It was probably ordered by William Blakiston Bowes.*

53. *The arms of the Bowes family as engraved in the centre of the dish.*

combined with 20 St James's Square, the house designed for Sir Watkin Williams Wynn by Robert Adam which Lord Strathmore leased from 1908 to 1920, must have been a heady stimulus to the Strathmores' youngest daughter. As David Bowes-Lyon told Lady Cynthia Asquith, he and his sister saw 'Glamis as a holiday place, Streatlam as a visit, and St Paul's as "Home"'.

To understand that more clearly and see how pictures and objects at Clarence House fit together, more must be said about the histories of the Bowes and Bowes-Lyon families.

The earliest family portrait is the Jacobean Lady Bowes, the wife of Sir Thomas Bowes (51), which Queen Elizabeth acquired in 1963. By normal rules of inheritance he should not have inherited Streatlam, but when his grandfather, Sir George, who died in 1580, married for a second time, he made a settlement in favour of the children of that marriage. Thus Thomas, who was his fourth but eldest surviving son of that second marriage, eventually came into Streatlam. He married Anne, daughter of Thomas Warcop of Tanfield, the presumed lady in the portrait, who lived until 1653. However in the family trees in Hutchinson's and Surtees's histories of Durham, as well as in modern ones, Thomas Bowes is not shown as a knight; but in the past there seems to have been a confusion between knighthoods for his brother, who died in 1638, and his elder son, both called Talbot. So is the portrait of his wife or Agnes Warcop who was married to Sir Talbot Bowes?

It was Thomas and Anne's grandson, William (baptized in 1656), who married Elizabeth Blakiston, the heiress to Gibside. Sir William died in 1706, leaving three sons, all minors, who succeeded him in turn. The eldest, William Blakiston Bowes, rebuilt Streatlam in 1717–18 and died at the age of 24 in 1721. He was followed in quick succession by his two brothers, Thomas, who was unmarried and died in 1722, and then by George, who was 21 at the time.

From this period there is a splendid memorial at Clarence House in the form of a great silver-gilt sideboard dish and ewer made by David Willaume in 1718 (52). The date suggests that it was bought by William Blakiston Bowes, but the arms (unusually showing all nine quarterings to which the family was entitled) could have been used by any of the brothers between that date and 1724. The arms suggest an awareness of history that fits with the rebuilding of Streatlam and the retention of the description 'Castle'.

However it is known that George bought plate because he gave a pair of flagons to the church at Whickham in 1722; at the time of his marriage in 1724, he also ordered a splendid kettle-on-stand, now in the Metropolitan Museum, New York, from Simon Pantin bearing his arms and those of his 14-year-old bride, Eleanor Verney, who died after only three months. Queen Elizabeth acquired in 1956 a bullet-shaped silver teapot-on-stand made by Francis Batty the Younger of Newcastle, that bears the Newcastle mark for 1722, and that is engraved with eight rather than nine quarterings of the Bowes arms (54).

The engraving of the arms on the sideboard dish (53) is of particularly fine quality and it can be compared with the arms on a smaller silver salver also by David Willaume of 1718, now in the Boston Museum of Fine Arts. It shows at the top left the three longbows of the Bowes family; in the middle the arms of Dalden, because Sir William Bowes married Maude, daughter and heiress of Robert de Dalden, about 1400; at the top right the arms are probably Trayne, Sir John Trayne of Streatlam having married Agnes Delahay in 1310; on the left in the middle row the arms are probably a Blakiston ancestor; in the centre the arms are Conyers, Sir Robert Bowes having married Joan Conyers in the early 15th century; on the right they are Aske, Richard Bowes having married Elizabeth Aske in 1558; the arms at bottom left are possibly Dautry; the centre ones are unidentified; and bottom right they are Blakiston, Sir William Bowes having married Elizabeth Blakiston in 1693.

Given that display, it is tantalizing not to be absolutely certain who acquired the dish and ewer. However that does not detract from the splendour of their design, the richness of the ornament and the contrast of textures.

After the dish and ewer were sold from Streatlam, they were acquired by William

ANCESTRY OF BOWES
OF STREATLAM

Sir Adam Bowes
Lord of Streatlam (*fl.* 1310–47)
Ancestor of

Sir George Bowes
Provost-Marshal North of the Trent (1527–80)

Sir William Bowes
Ambassador to Scotland (*d.* 1611)

George Bowes
of Biddick (*d.* 1606)

Sir Talbot Bowes
of Streatlam and Aske, MP
for Richmond (*d.* 1638) *d.s.p.*

Thomas Bowes = Anne, dau. of
(*fl.* 1600–1607)   Thomas Warcop

Talbot Bowes
(1603–54)

Thomas Bowes
(1607–61)

Sir William Bowes = Elizabeth, dau. of Sir Francis
(1656–1706)   Blakiston of Gibside

William Blakiston Bowes
(1697–1721) *d.s.p.*

Thomas Bowes
(*d.* 1722) *d.s.p.*

(1) Eleanor, dau. of =
Hon. Thomas Verney

George Bowes
of Streatlam and Gibside (1701–60)

= (2) Mary, dau. of Edward Gilbert

Mary Eleanor Bowes = John Lyon, 9th Earl of Strathmore
(1749–1800)

ANCESTRY OF
THE EARLS OF
STRATHMORE

Sir John Lyon of Forteviot and Glamis
granted Thanage of Glamis by Robert II (*d.* 1382)
Ancestor of

Patrick, 3rd Earl
created Earl of Strathmore and Kinghorne, 1677 (1643–95)

John, 4th Earl = Elizabeth, dau. of Earl of Chesterfield
(1663–1712)

John, 5th Earl
(1690–1715) *d.s.p.*

Charles, 6th Earl
(1699–1728) *d.s.p.*

James, 7th Earl
(1702–35) *d.s.p.*

Thomas, 8th Earl
(1704–53)

John, 9th Earl   =
assumed surname of
Bowes 1767 (1737–76)

Mary Eleanor Bowes
(*see Bowes Pedigree*)

James Lyon
(1738–63)

Thomas Lyon
(1741–96)

John, 10th Earl   =
created Baron Bowes of Streatlam
Castle and Lunedale, 1815 (1769–1820)

Mary, dau. of J. Milner
of Stainton

Thomas, 11th Earl
(1773–1846)

John Bowes
(1811–85)

Thomas George Bowes
(1801–34)

Thomas George, 12th Earl
(1822–65) *d.s.p.*

Claude, 13th Earl
created Baron Bowes of Streatlam
Castle and Lundale, 1887 (1824–1904)

Claude, 14th Earl   =
(1855–1944)

Nina, dau. of Rev.
Charles Cavendish-Bentinck

Violet Hyacinth
Bowes-Lyon
(1882–93)

Patrick, 15th Earl
(1884–1949)

Alexander Francis
Bowes-Lyon
(1887–1911)

Rose Constance
Bowes-Lyon
(1890–1967)

ELIZABETH
ANGELA MARGUERITE
BOWES-LYON
(*b.* 1900)

Mary Frances
Bowes-Lyon
(1883–1961)

John Herbert
Bowes-Lyon
(1886–1930)

Fergus
Bowes-Lyon
(1889–1911)

Michael
Bowes-Lyon
(1893–1953)

David
Bowes-Lyon
(1902–61)

John, Master of Glamis
(killed in action, 1941)

Timothy Patrick,
16th Earl
(1918–72)

Fergus, 17th Earl
(1928–87)

Michael, 18th Earl
(*b.* 1957)

Randolph Hearst for St Donat's Castle in Wales and were resold at Christie's in 1938. Presumably then or soon after, they were acquired by the Queen, but there is no record of their purchase.

After the death of his wife, George Bowes withdrew to Gibside, where he concentrated on his mining developments along the Derwent, a tributary of the Tyne, and on transforming the landscape into one of the most famous in the north of England.

It was not until 1743 that he married again. His second wife was Mary Gilbert, the heiress to St Paul's Walden Bury. Right at the end of his life he commissioned James Paine to design the chapel and mausoleum at Gibside, but that was still not finished when he died in 1760.

His only daughter, Mary Eleanor, who was just 11 at the time, was a great heir-

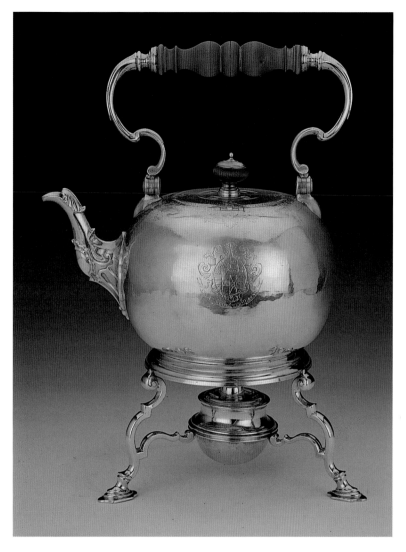

54. *A bullet-shaped tea-kettle and stand with the Bowes crest, by Francis Batty, with the Newcastle date stamp for 1722.*

ess. In 1767 she married the 9th Earl of Strathmore, whose father had died in 1753 and whose mother came from Co. Durham. It was a grand match, but her mother was right to recognize that they were not well suited to each other. Despite five children the marriage proved unsatisfactory, and, when in 1776 Lord Strathmore had to go off to Lisbon on what proved a fruitless attempt to recover his health (he was suffering from tuberculosis), he was worried about what would happen to his wife and their children, particularly his elder son whom she disliked. Lord Strathmore died at sea.

Within the year Lady Strathmore, who was a talented linguist and botanist, made a disastrous second marriage to an adventurer called Andrew Stoney who called himself Bowes. He could not get his hands on her money, which was in trust, and so in revenge he sold her possessions, cut down her trees and treated her with great cruelty. Eventually she escaped through divorce in 1789, but he remained in debt until his death, under the watchful eye of the King's Bench prison.

The Strathmores had had two sons: John, who became 10th Earl and whose full-length portrait by the American painter, Mather Brown (55), hangs in the Upper Corridor; and Thomas, who successfully claimed the Earldom on the 10th Earl's death in 1820. The dashing 10th Earl came of age in 1790, bought out his mother's life interest in Streatlam and restored the estates, as well as completing the chapel at Gibside. He is depicted in uniform, possibly of the Gibside Cavalry (later known as the Derwent and Gibside Yeomanry), a troop that he raised during the Napoleonic War.

The 10th Earl also greatly enjoyed the theatricals organized at Seaton Delaval, the great house by Vanbrugh on the other side of Newcastle from Gibside. There he fell in love with Lord Delaval's daughter, Sarah, who as a minor had married the 2nd Earl of Tyrconnel. In 1791 John and Sarah went off together. She died at Gibside in 1800.

Nine years after Lady Tyrconnel's death, Lord Strathmore met Mary Millner, who worked on one of his properties near Streatlam. In 1811 she had a son whom they called John Bowes and whom Lord Strathmore always acknowledged. From about 1812 or 1813 Mary lived as Lord Strathmore's wife at Streatlam, the boy being called Lord Glamis (114). In a last-minute attempt to legitimize him and secure the Strathmore succession for him, Lord Strathmore married Mary Millner on 2 July 1820 at St George's, Hanover Square. The following day he died. Whereas under English law such a marriage could not make a child legitimate, it could under Scottish law and that was the case made on behalf of John Bowes. However his claim was challenged in the Committee of Privileges of the House of Lords by the 10th Earl's younger brother, Thomas, on the ground that it was an English contract made in England and the couple were domiciled in England. He won and was accepted as 11th Earl and obtained Glamis, but he was not able to upset his brother's will leaving Streatlam and Gibside to his son and his heirs, with the proviso that if he had no children the properties would return to the main line.

The 10th Earl's widow, Mary, Lady Strathmore, lived on until 1860, and she was outlived by her second husband, William Hutt, who had been John Bowes's tutor at Cambridge. Hutt continued to live at Gibside until 1874.

John Bowes grew up to be by any standards a remarkable man, a Member of Parliament, a landowner with extensive coal and shipping interests, a leading figure in racing (76), as will be seen in the Horse Corridor at Clarence House, a theatrical proprietor in Paris and also the creator of one of the most unexpected museums in England, the Bowes Museum at Barnard Castle. He is also the most intriguing character in the history of the family because of the combination of his achievements and interests and the accident of his birth. Having been brought up as his father's heir and sent to Eton, it must have been exceedingly difficult to accept his altered position,

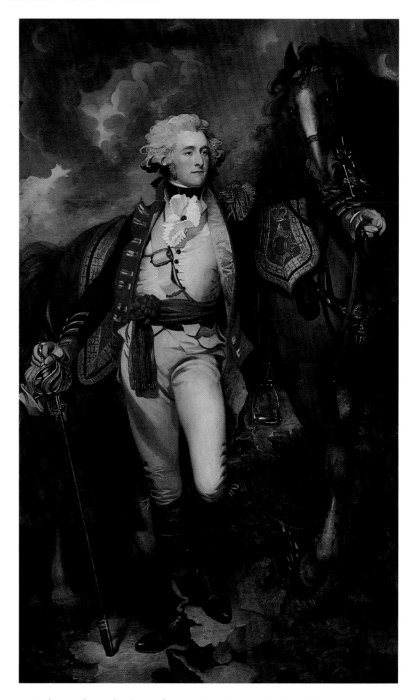

55. The 10th Earl of Strathmore (*1764–1820*) *by Mather Brown* (*a portrait in the Upper Corridor*).

55

but he pressed on to do all that an early-19th-century landowner was expected to do. Thus, having been appointed a Deputy Lieutenant at the age of 20, as soon as he came of age he was elected to Parliament for the first time; and in 1835 he won his first Derby.

However he never seems to have completely settled into that conventional kind of upper-class life; Paris, where he may have gone for the first time in 1832 and where he became a member of the Jockey Club in 1835, and its theatrical life seems to have had a stronger pull. In 1846 he took a house in Paris and also bought the Théâtre des Variétés, which proved an unfortunately costly enterprise for the next 12 years. In 1847 he met a young French actress, Josephine Benoite Coffin-Chevallier, and decided to settle in Paris, giving up his seat in Parliament. However he continued to race and in 1852 served his year as High Sheriff. In 1852 he and Josephine had a civil marriage in Paris and that was followed up by an Anglican marriage in London in 1854. By then they had started to collect works of art, initially to furnish Madame du Barry's château at Louveciennes, which he gave his wife as a wedding present, and that enthusiasm gathered pace after they moved to 7 rue de Berlin in 1857.

The following year Mrs Bowes came with him to Streatlam and Gibside for the first time. About 1864 they began to think about founding a museum near Streatlam, at the time a highly original concept because such institutions outside London were still in their infancy, and they proposed to set up and fund a French-style museum on the scale worthy of a major French provincial town. In 1865 Mrs Bowes bought the site on the edge of Barnard Castle out of some of the proceeds of her sale of the house at Louveciennes and building began four years later. Sadly she died in 1874, but, despite all the difficulties, John Bowes pressed on with the project. Thus by the time he died in 1885 Barnard Castle was dominated by its overscale Renaissance Revival château.

Not surprisingly John Bowes had had little contact with the 11th Earl of Strathmore who had disinherited him, nor with his son, who died in 1865. However he had established friendly relations with the 13th Earl, the brother of the 12th, and the Strathmores used to stay at Streatlam.

John Bowes was careful not to leave to his museum any Bowes heirlooms and so on his death they, together with Streatlam and Gibside, went back to the main Bowes-Lyon line, to Queen Elizabeth's grandfather.

A TOUR OF
CLARENCE HOUSE

WHEN THE BLACK gates of Clarence House swing back, Queen Elizabeth or her guests find themselves almost immediately under the portico, with the door on the left. So, although many visitors coming on business use the Household entrance on the north side of the house and come into the Hall through the door under the stairs at the north end, it is at the main, south door that this tour begins.

The Outer Hall

The Outer Hall was added on in the 1870s, when the Duke of Edinburgh rebuilt most of the south end of the house and extended the hall by one bay. Here the visitor is greeted by one of Queen Elizabeth's enthusiasms: clocks. Clarence House is full of clocks – English clocks, French clocks, clocks by country makers, long-case clocks, bracket clocks – and most rooms have several. The most extraordinary of all, however, is the musical clock (56–8) whose design must be inspired by the crown spire of St Giles's Cathedral, Edinburgh, which has come (quite wrongly) to be thought of as a Scottish idea, but made Gothic Revival. Most visitors only see its main face, now facing west, which has dials for seconds, days, and months as well as the hours, and another for music or silence, but the other sides are just as interesting. The 'south' face

56. The musical clock by John Smith of Pittenweem, 1804.

57

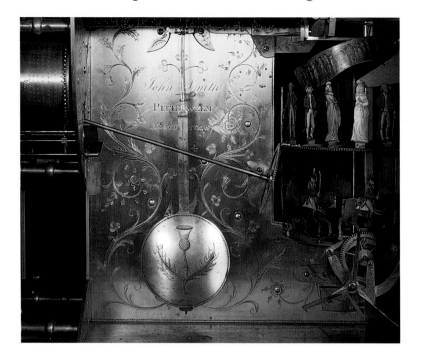

57. *Detail of the back plate of the clock with the maker's name and date.*

records the sixteen tunes that it plays: they include 'My Nanie O' and the 'East Nook of Fife', as well as 'God Save the King' and the '100 Psalm' tune – but it was silent 'in Remembrance of the Sabbath'. On the 'east face', which is the back (57), the maker's plate can be seen and also some of the figures that appear on the 'north' face. That consists of a classical palace with an open central doorway across which passes a procession of royal figures; below there is a moving mounted guard and sentries; a royal carriage procession is painted at the bottom and a Royal Arms painted in the arched sky at the top (58).

Sadly this clock is no longer in full working order, but, if it was, surely some people would be late for audiences. Perhaps only its size and delicacy explains why it has never been loaned to an exhibition and therefore is so little known.

The clock was made in 1804 in Pittenweem, on the coast of Fife, by John Smith, who worked there from 1770 to 1814. All the decorative painting was done by Alexander Naysmith (1758–1840), one of the leading Scottish landscape painters of his day, a friend of Robert Burns and a scientific enthusiast – which presumably explains how he came to collaborate with Smith. When first exhibited in 1804, the clock did not find a purchaser and was eventually sold by lottery in 1809. It was a wedding present to the Duke and Duchess of York from the citizens of Glasgow.

Three steps from the Outer Hall lead up to glazed double doors that open on the long Hall.

58. *One side of the clock with the procession of royal figures that moves across the central doorway and below the moving mounted guard and sentries.*

The Hall

Nash's corridor, which he planned as running behind his main rooms, together with its corresponding upper version, now provide the spines to the house. It is fortunate that no one since the 1870s has tried to articulate it with columns or cross arches, as that would have made the north end even darker. Instead Queen Elizabeth has treated both as galleries for pictures, varied with tapestry and looking-glasses, and given form by the full-length portraits on the west walls that answer the arches on the east walls. This is skilfully done, because the odd building history of the house means that nothing on the west and east walls actually quite lines up.

Each bay is now made to tell a different story, while the eye is led onward along the succession of rugs on the red carpet towards the Staircase.

Thus, looking left first, there is a Brussels tapestry woven about 1600, which Queen Elizabeth acquired in 1950 (59). It is of a garden with arbours seen through a colonnade with a figure of Flora or Pomona, and a gardener in the centre and deer in the outer bays. The side scenes with their arcades are derived from a tapestry in a set of garden panels woven for Cardinal Granvella in the 1560s and now in the Kunsthistorisches Museum, Vienna, but the middle scene has been altered. It appears that at some stage the top of this tapestry has been slightly trimmed.

The way the tapestry is placed here is effective not only because it creates a sense of architecture with an illusion of space and recession, but also because the low tones of faded greens, blues and fawns with only a little rose seem to bring the garden outside into the house.

In front of the tapestry stand a pair of tall Sèvres jars given to the King and Queen on their state visit to France in 1938. While the blue is characteristic of Sèvres, the art deco treatment of shooting scenes, with men riding in howdahs on the backs of elephants and camels in the jungle, seems a surprising official souvenir.

At the end of the bay, just by the Morning Room door but behind the lamp, hangs the sketch of Queen Elizabeth in Garter robes painted by Simon Elwes (62) (1902–75) in 1951 when he was also working on the big picture on the east wall

59. The Hall with a Brussels tapestry of about 1600.

that was completed in 1953. Here the King is seen investing Princess Elizabeth with the Insignia of the Order of the Garter at a Chapter of the Order held in the Throne Room at Windsor Castle on 23 April 1948 (61). To the left of it hangs a sketch of Queen Alexandra by Edward Hughes, and on the right is another, smaller sketch by Sir David Wilkie (1785–1841) of George IV painted in preparation for *The Entry of George IV into Holyrood* commemorating the first visit of a British sovereign to Scotland since Charles II was crowned at Scone in 1651 (64). The picture, which was finally completed in 1830, is now at Holyrood. The sketch was recommended by Anthony Blunt, the Surveyor of the King's Pictures, and acquired by Queen Elizabeth in 1948. Here George IV seems about to stride into the Garter picture. It is a witty piece of juxtaposition, but there is more to it than that.

Not only was the Garter ceremony of deep personal significance to the King, the Queen, the Princess and the Duke of Edinburgh (who was made a Knight Companion on that occasion), but it was also the 600th anniversary of the foundation of the Order and the first Chapter held since the Second World War. (The previous April the King and Queen had been on their South African tour.) The picture shows the Queen seated on the left, and to the right of her stand the Duke of Norfolk, the Duke of Devonshire and the Earl of Halifax, with Princess Elizabeth facing the King, and Sir Algar Howard, Garter Principal King of Arms, standing between them. To the right of the King is Eric Hamilton, Dean of Windsor and Registrar of the Order, and on the far right are Vice-Admiral Sir Geoffrey Blake, Gentleman Usher of the Black Rod, and the Bishop of Winchester, Prelate of the Order. It was on that occasion that the gift of the Order of the Garter was formally restored to the Sovereign, the Prime Minister relinquishing any say in who was to be honoured. Two preparatory sketches for the King's portrait hang upstairs, one appearing in Plate 110 and the other (63), which is complementary to that of the Queen, is in Queen Elizabeth's Sitting Room.

The Garter picture should not be looked at in isolation at Clarence House, however, because it is part of a chronological story that reflects the intensity of the period in which Queen Elizabeth was most active in acquiring pictures by living artists: the increasingly menacing situation in the late 1930s when the years of

60. *Looking-glass flanked by portraits of Queen Charlotte and King George III, with a* Directoire *clock flanked by Louis Seize porphyry vases.*

61. Left King George VI investing Princess Elizabeth with the Insignia of the Order of the Garter in the Throne Room at Windsor Castle on April 23, 1948 *by Simon Elwes. The picture was completed in 1953.*
62. & 63. Below left *Sketches of King George VI and Queen Elizabeth for the Garter picture.*
64. Right *A preparatory sketch of King George IV for* The Entry of George IV into Holyrood *by Sir David Wilkie.*

war threatened not only Britain but civilization, and the hard, grey years immediately afterwards. There is surely something doubly celebratory about the Garter picture, and that sense becomes even stronger after seeing other pictures and sculptures in the house. That first becomes apparent with the pictures of Windsor Castle by John Piper (74) in the adjoining Lancaster Room, painted at a time when the Castle might well have been bombed. It is strengthened with Augustus John's portrait of the Queen in the Garden Room (81): about which she wrote to him in 1942: 'If you are still in London, I could come to your studio if you have any windows, for we have none in Buckingham Palace, and it is too dark and dusty to paint in anyway.' And it continues even more forcibly with Sir Winston Churchill's bust (88) by Sir William Reid-Dick placed among the formal garniture on the Morning Room chimneypiece and the fine picture of *Field Marshal Montgomery in his HQ Mess Tent in Belgium in 1944* by Sir James Gunn at the foot of the staircase (72).

On the other side of the door to the Lancaster Room are smaller portraits of King George III from the circle of Francis Cotes and of Queen Charlotte by a follower of George Knapton, which were given to King George VI when Duke of York by Queen Mary. They flank one of a pair of gilded looking-glasses with unusually pronounced capitals and other interesting detail that suggests a date about 1730 (60). The glasses do not feel like London work and, since they are supposed to have come from Newbattle Abbey, formerly the principal house of the Marquesses of Lothian near Edinburgh, it is tempting to wonder whether they

65. Left *King George III when Prince of Wales: a studio version of Allan Ramsay's portrait painted in 1758. On the left is a small portrait of Queen Charlotte and a plaster figure of King George III, and on the right a bust of King George VI by Sir William Reid-Dick, 1943.*
66. Above *A southward view of the Hall from the Staircase with a companion portrait of Augusta Princess of Wales.*

67

67. Newhaven Pier *by Duncan Grant. It was acquired in 1939.*

could be by a Scottish carver. The glasses, which were possibly found by Sir Arthur Penn, were bought by the Queen in 1942.

On the marble-top table is one of a pair of *Directoire* chinoiserie clocks signed by Denis-François Dubois, and a handsome pair of Louis Seize porphyry vases that incorporate gilt portrait medals by Dassier of Frederick Prince of Wales and the 2nd Duke of Argyll. With them are recent arrivals, including casts of Chinese tomb figures that Queen Elizabeth acquired at a Chinese exhibition.

The next facing bay between the Morning Room and Library doors is mostly devoted to King George III, with a studio version of Allan Ramsay's portrait of the King when Prince of Wales. It was painted for the Earl of Bute in 1758 and is still in the Bute Collection at Mount Stuart, in Scotland (65). Queen Elizabeth bought it at the Earl of Home's sale of pictures from The Hirsel near Berwick-on-Tweed at Christie's in 1948. On the left of it is a small portrait of Queen Charlotte by Thomas Frye hanging over a plaster figure of George III by an unknown sculptor, and on the right is a bust of King George VI done in 1943 by Sir William Reid-Dick (1879–1961). Reid-Dick had made the tomb of King George V and

Queen Mary in St George's Chapel at Windsor Castle and had then done their memorials at Sandringham and Crathie, as well as the statue of King George V in London. In 1938 he became Sculptor to the King and subsequently served the present Queen.

The portrait of George III when Prince of Wales is balanced by a studio version of Ramsay's portrait of his mother, Augusta Princess of Wales, which is also at Mount Stuart (66). Queen Mary acquired the picture for Marlborough House and then borrowed the George III to go with it.

The almost facing group in the bay between the two arches has the second Newbattle glass but changes character in its flanking pictures in a way that is a hallmark of the house: here is a Duncan Grant of *Newhaven Pier* (67) bought in 1939 and a small painting of *A Girl in Pink Leaning on a Chair* by Alfred Stevens (1823–1906) (68). Despite his very English-sounding name, Stevens was born in Brussels and, although not an Impressionist himself, he was a friend of Manet and Berthe Morisot and used to hang pictures by them in his studio in the hope that he would make sales to his patrons. Indeed it was in his studio that Durand Ruel saw the first two Manets that he bought. Queen Elizabeth bought the picture in 1942.

Beyond the second arch is a large cabinet containing part of a Worcester service made about 1795 that, according to tradition, George IV gave to the King of Hanover (69,70). The tradition dates from the Christie's sale catalogue of 1900, but there is no documentary proof in the Royal Archives. After King George III and Queen Charlotte visited Worcester to attend the Three Choirs Festival in 1788, the King gave Flight a Royal Warrant and the firm received an order from the Duke of Clarence for a service to cost £700. By then John Pennington had become Worcester's principal painter and it was he who painted the Hanover service.

In 1900, 176 pieces from that service were sold at Christie's and then in 1941 fifty-two

68. A Girl in Pink Leaning on a Chair *by Alfred Stevens*.

69

69. *Cabinet containing part of the Hanover service.*

pieces appeared in Lady Daresbury's sale at Sotheby's. Queen Elizabeth bought them and over the years she has acquired more of the service, but, as invariably happens, that has become more difficult – and expensive – as the years go by.

The pictures at the far end of the corridor take a step back in time. Here at the foot of the stairs is the portrait of Prince James Francis Edward and his sister Princess Louisa Maria Theresa by Nicolas de Largillière (1656–1746) (71). It was the birth of the Prince in June 1688 that led to the revolution of 1688 and the flight of James II. The children were brought up at St Germain-en-Laye near Paris and the first version of the picture (now in the National Portrait Gallery) was painted there in 1695. The Prince became the Old Pretender and died in 1719; his sister died in 1712. Those sad figures whom Queen Elizabeth's Lyon ancestors loyally supported and her Bowes ancestors opposed have intrigued her since childhood, as is known from the reminiscence of the Minister at Glamis recounted on page 23. Queen Elizabeth bought the picture at the sale of pictures belonging to her brother-in-law, Lord Elphinstone, in 1965.

On the end wall is a portrait by Sir Peter Lely (1618–80) of Prince Rupert of the Rhine, the son of Elizabeth Queen of Bohemia and Frederick V, the Elector Palatine.

Beside it is a picture that brings back the Second World War with unexpected force and in an unexpected way: the conversation piece of *Field Marshal Montgomery in his Mess Tent in Belgium in 1944* by James Gunn (1893–1964) (72). It shows on the left the Field Marshal in flying jacket and corduroy trousers with Lt Col. C.P. Dawnay, who was a Military Assistant; Captain Rae Bon Durrant, USA, who was an American Liaison Officer, standing; Captain Johnny Henderson, the ADC; Captain Noel Chavasse, a Liaison Officer, seen from behind; and Lt Col. Trumbull Warren, a Canadian Liaison Officer.

Early in 1944 Montgomery had sat to Augustus John for a portrait, and, although that was not a success, there is a fascinating drawing of him sitting, with Bernard Shaw looking on, which must have been done by Gunn later, because he did not meet Montgomery until he went to France in August that year. It seems that Montgomery had admired portraits by Gunn in the Royal Academy in 1944, and, when the *Sunday Despatch* wanted to commission a portrait of him to present to his mother, he suggested that Gunn should paint it.

Exceptionally for him, Gunn wrote a graphic account of that visit from 28 August to 19 September 1944, of which a typed copy is now placed behind the picture. Since it is too long to quote in full, here are some of the references that have most bearing on the picture.

Monday 28th August ... Right away I met the great man and I felt we clicked, he took me in to the map room and showed me what had been done and what was going to be done. When I had settled in to the caravan we had tea. I met the ADCs, Johnny Henderson, Capt. Chavasse, Col. Warren Canadian and a Yankee, all young and how the C-in-C rags them ...

Wednesday 30th ... These youngsters are given their heads at dinner time, say what they like and M. loves it, he won't have seniors at his mess, this way he gets clear of the

70. *Pieces from the Hanover service. Made at Worcester about 1795, it was painted by John Pennington.*

71. *Prince James Francis Edward Stuart, the Old Pretender, and his sister, Princess Louisa Maria Theresa by Nicolas de Largillière, about 1695.*

business at intervals, his recreation, the place is a menagerie, rabbits with their young and the dogs, Hitler, Rommel, Keitel and another, canaries and chickens and they all move around with the convoy.

Friday 1st September Chief has been made Field Marshal . . .

Saturday 2nd . . . After tea started work on small Con. Piece in the mess. Sitting again at 6 til 7. Light difficult, and changeable but no good complaining just got to do it anyway. Trum came in and looked at the new picture, wildly enthusiastic, I think I've got something . . .

Sunday 10th . . . Started study of Johnny for Con. Piece . . .

Friday 15th Sitting from Rae got him in to the picture standing up behind.

Saturday 16th . . . Worked like mad all day, Rae from 9 to 11, Chief from 11 to 1, Trum 2 to 3, Chief 3 to 4, Johnnie 4.30–6 and Trum 6 to 7.30 feeling much better.

Sunday 17th . . . I painted on Rae and Noel, changed the whole attitude of N. much better . . .

Monday 18th . . . C of S came to lunch thrilled with picture of chief and also with small Con. Piece. I won't know what either are like till I get them home . . .

72. Field Marshal Montgomery in his HQ Mess Tent in Belgium in 1944 *by James Gunn.*

Tues 19th Last day. Worked on Con. Piece. Boulogne confirmed. Guards Div. going forward at great speed. Eindhoven relieved. Rae sat then the Chief 11.30–12.30. Trum after lunch then Kit then Johnnie. C of S and Miles Graham came and said goodbye ...

Montgomery was thrilled with the portrait that Gunn painted of him and in a letter to Sir Alan Lascelles dated 20 September 1944, he mentioned the conversation picture, saying that it would be going down to his house in the country with the portrait and that the King might like to see it: 'he would know the characters so well'. In fact Montgomery did not acquire the picture, and the artist sent it to the Royal Academy in 1945. There it was seen by the Queen, who asked whether it was available and was told Montgomery did not want it. So she bought it as a war picture by a living artist. However, later Montgomery changed his mind and tried hard to get the picture from the Queen. Naturally she would not agree to that and in the end Gunn painted a second version for him.

The Lancaster Room

This room owes its name to its chimneypiece that was acquired from the wedding present fund given by the people of Lancashire to Princess Elizabeth and the Duke of Edinburgh. The chimneypiece originally came from the house in St Stephen's Green, Dublin, built by the 2nd Lord Brandon in 1765, but it was taken out long ago. Its last home before Clarence House was a house in Lowndes Square.

Princess Elizabeth used the room as a waiting room, and this continues. It is here people wait before audiences with Queen Elizabeth, which are usually held in the Morning Room.

However its visual point is the double set of twenty-six views of Windsor Castle, Frogmore and Virginia Water by John Piper that was the Queen's most ambitious and important commission (73, 74). Originally planned in 1941, the first set was completed in 1942 and the second in 1944. Some of them are familiar from exhibitions and reproduction, but the impact of the whole set must be especially intense to someone of the Queen's generation.

By the late 1930s John Piper was growing out of his phase of abstract painting and also, as a result of meeting John Betjeman in 1937, he was writing about and photographing architecture for the *Shell Guide to Oxfordshire*. Thus by 1939 his response in painting to English architecture was becoming increasingly strong. By 1941 he had developed his topographical style in which accurately rendered buildings were treated in a romantic way with dramatic lighting and landscape settings. Sir Kenneth Clark had begun to buy his work in 1939 and was determined to secure work for him through the newly created War Artists Advisory Committee when he set it up that year. Thus in November 1940 John Piper was sent to record the bombed Coventry Cathedral and the following year to draw blitzed churches in Bristol. In the summer of 1941 Sir Kenneth organized an exhibition of pictures at the National Gallery for the 'Recording Britain' project, financed by the Pilgrim Trust, and to this the Queen went. The Queen already had it in mind to commission a set of views of Windsor Castle, and Sir Kenneth suggested to her that Piper should be asked to do it. As she has said, she did not know whether Windsor would come through the war and at least there would be a record of it. So the stormy lighting seems to reflect the mood of the times when they were done, and surely Wyatville's rather hard remodelling of the castle has never looked more dramatic and powerful.

73. *The views of Windsor Castle, Frogmore and Virginia Water by John Piper in the Lancaster Room.*

74. Overleaf
Four views by John Piper: (above left) The West End of the Upper Ward with the Round Tower; (below left) The View from the Middle Ward with the Winchester Tower with St George's Chapel and the Lower Ward; (above right) The Brunswick Tower Overlooking Home Park; (below right) The Horseshoe Cloister and the Curfew Tower.

The earliest dated reference to the commission is in a letter from Sir Jasper Ridley to John Piper on 9 July 1941. Sir Jasper mentioned the painter's semi-abstract *Approach to Fonthill*, which he had bought at the Leicester Galleries a year earlier, but the main point of his letter was to further a scheme that John Piper should go up to Blagdon in Northumberland to stay with Lady Ridley, Sir Jasper's niece by marriage (and the daughter of Sir Edwin Lutyens) and paint. 'That Northumberland country, if you happen to catch its atmosphere, is magnificent; Seaton Delaval is about nine or ten miles from Blagdon, and should give you scope. The Roman wall, of course, is sure to stir up your imagination, if it needs stirring up.' Proof of the success of the expedition is to be seen in pictures of Seaton Delaval acquired by Sir Kenneth Clark and the Tate Gallery.

Just a month later, on 15 August, Sir Kenneth wrote to John Piper:

Dear John, This is to confirm our conversation yesterday in which I told you of the Queen's commission to paint a series of watercolours of Windsor Castle and Great Park. We agreed that you would do fifteen water colours for £150, this sum to include expenses. I have written to the Librarian, Owen Morshead, telling him about the commission and that you will be calling on him soon. I know he will do everything he can to help you.

That is the only price given for one of the Queen's purchases in this book, and is included as a counter to the impression of the munificence of the commission and as an indicator of prices that rising artists expected to receive at that time and collectors were used to paying. And if it seems unbelievable now, it has to be related to the costs of daily life at the time.

On 21 August John Piper wrote to John Betjeman: 'I follow unworthily in the footsteps of Paul Sandby, who did two hundred watercolours for George III, which I am instructed to look at earnestly before starting.'

The Queen's feeling when she commissioned the watercolours is now very strongly brought to mind by the small bronze group under one of them. It shows firefighters at work and was given to Her Majesty by the Firefighters Memorial Trust when she unveiled the Blitz Memorial on 4 May 1991. Beside it is a special decoration devised by the crew of the *Ark Royal* with bars on a ribbon that commemorate the Queen's six visits to the ship.

On two of the walls, Piper's pictures have highly burnished water gilt frames but the remainder still have their original simple spoon utility mouldings – all that was available during the War.

The Horse Corridor

Queen Elizabeth's love of racing has given a great deal of pleasure and excitement to many other people over several decades, but what may come as a surprise is to see in the Horse Corridor the extent to which hers is an inherited enthusiasm (75). In fact the earliest recorded win in her family appears to be in 1622 when Sir George Bowes of Streatlam won a race on Richmond Moor. The early-18th-century William Blakiston Bowes started a stud at Streatlam through buying a mare by Byerly Turk, and his youngest brother, George, took an active part in developing racing in the north of England, particularly at Newcastle. Both the 5th and 9th Earls of Strathmore bred horses. The 10th Earl entered a horse for the Derby in 1793, and in 1795 re-established the Streatlam stud by walking five horses all the way from Esher in Surrey to Co. Durham. He bought Queen Mab and through her established one of the two main lines that continued for many years, producing Remembrancer which won the St Leger in 1803. However the most successful breeder and racing man in the family was John Bowes, his natural son, who won the Derby no less than four times.

John Bowes's success was built on his father's stud, which his trustees had kept going during his minority. As soon as he came of age in 1832, he appointed Isaac Walker as his stud groom and soon after asked John Scott of Whitewell near Malton, in Yorkshire, to become his trainer. Between 1827 and 1864 John Scott, known as 'The Wizard of the North', trained six winners of the Derby, eight of the Oaks, sixteen of the St Leger and eight of the 2000 Guineas. John Bowes's first great success was to win the Derby in 1835, with Mundig, a horse that came from his father's second – Beatrice – line, and had never raced at all. Mundig was the first horse he had entered for a race in the south of England and was also the first northern horse to win the race.

By 1839 John Bowes had eleven horses running, and that year he entered them for forty races all over England – a considerable feat considering they still had to walk to meetings.

His second triumph was with Cotherstone, another horse in the Beatrice line, which he began to race in 1842. Cotherstone won both the 2000 Guineas and the Derby in 1843, only just failing to win the Triple Crown through a case of suspect riding. In 1963 Queen Elizabeth bought the celebration picture painted by J.F. Herring (1795–1865) (76) with the winner in the middle with W. Scott up.

75. *The Horse Corridor looking west towards the Hall.*

Around it in the luxuriant Rococo Revival frame are, on the left, Gibside Fairy, his granddam and dam of Emma; Whisker, his grandsire, which won the Derby in 1815 and was sire of Emma; and Emma, his dam; and on the right Whalebone, his great grandsire, which won the Derby in 1810 and was the sire of Camel; Camel, his grandsire and sire of Touchstone; and Touchstone, the winner of the St Leger in 1834 and his sire.

Close by are other portraits of Cotherstone by Herring and W. B. Barraud (*c*.1810–50), which Queen Elizabeth bought in 1973.

John Bowes's two other triumphs are represented here. In 1852 he won the Derby yet again with Daniel O'Rourke, a horse in the Queen Mab line, which was painted by Thomas Bretland. Then in 1853 he won the race with West Australian, which also won the Triple Crown. The horse, which was in the Beatrice line, was painted by Harry Hall (recorded 1838–68) with John Scott who trained him, his head stable lad and Frank Butler who rode him in all his races.

76. *Cotherstone, John Bowes's second Derby winner in 1843, with his forebears by J.F. Herring: on the left are Gibside Fairy, Whisker and Emma, and on the right Whalebone, Camel and Touchstone.*

On the opposite wall is a smaller group of pictures connected with the 12th Earl of Strathmore. There is a brilliant sketch of him on horseback by Herring (77), which Queen Elizabeth acquired in 1957, and also the same artist's small oval sketches of him and Jem Mason in 1846 done for *Steeple Chase Cracks*. Jem Mason won the Grand National in 1839. With them is Herring's *Steeple Chase Cracks*, which shows a field of twelve taking a jump in a point-to-point, including Lord Strathmore on Switcher.

There is also a painting by H.B. Chalon (1771–1849) of a favourite horse and groom that belonged to Princess Charlotte in 1816, which was given by Queen Mary to King George VI in 1937.

77. *The 12th Earl of Strathmore, a sketch by J.F. Herring.*

78. *Some of Queen Elizabeth's horses: on the left is Makaldar, 1969; in the centre Double Star;
and below* The Rip Going Down at Cheltenham, *all by Pieter Biegel; on the right is Laffy,
Double Star and The Rip; and below that Susan Crawford's* Horse and Hound *cover from 1984
which depicts Fulke Walwyn, who trained for Her Majesty in the 1980s.*

These pictures naturally lead on to a group of pictures of some of Queen
Elizabeth's horses that hang at the east end of the corridor, at the foot of the
stairs (78). On the left is Pieter Biegel's pictures of Makaldar in 1969, with a
sketch of Double Star in the centre and below it *The Rip Going Down at Cheltenham*
painted in 1962. On the right there is a picture of Laffy, Double Star and
The Rip that commemorates their success for Queen Elizabeth when they all three
won races on the same day at Lingfield in January 1961. Below that is a 1984
cover design for *Horse and Hound* by Susan Crawford.

The Garden Room

The Garden Room, which was formed out of two rooms and transformed into a drawing room after Princess Margaret married in 1960, invariably seems to be sunny (80). That is partly its aspect, but also comes from the way the light is filtered through the sun curtains: meeting in the centre, they are held back and framed by the main curtains, which are in pale apricot with valances of green decorated with drapery of apricot lined with green. The light then plays on the 18th-century French carpet with bunches and sprays of flowers and the Royal Arms of France and Navarre in tones of faded purple, rose, apricot, green, blue, gold and white on a pale ground.

The room appears to be arranged around the portrait of Queen Elizabeth painted by Augustus John (1878–1961) (80,81). When it finally arrived at Clarence House in 1961 after it had fallen out of sight for twenty years, Queen Elizabeth wrote to the artist: 'I want to tell you what a tremendous pleasure it gives me to see it once again. It looks so lovely in my drawing-room, and has cheered it up no end! The sequins glitter, and the roses and the red chair give a fine glow, and I am so happy to have it ...'

The Queen, who was a long-standing admirer of the artist, enjoyed sitting to Augustus, as she refers to him, and her charming letter passes over the long and agonizing story of the commission that is told by Michael Holroyd in the second volume of his biography of Augustus John, *The Years of Experience* (1975). That deserves to be recounted here, albeit in a shortened form, because it is so rare to have that kind of record of a commission. John had first been suggested as a royal portrait painter in 1925 by Lord D'Abernon. Not surprisingly the Court turned down the idea. The King's private secretary replied: 'No! H.M. wouldn't look at A.J!! And so A.J. wouldn't be able to look at H.M!!' And no more was said until 1937 when Hugo Pitman invited John to meet the new Queen – provided he arrived dead sober – and the possibility of a portrait was raised. Nothing, however, happened, but the idea was not forgotten, and in 1939 John wrote to Maud Cazalet, a friend of the Queen: 'It is very nice to know that the Queen still wants

79. One of a pair of Chinese mirror-glass paintings in gilded Rococo frames and, below, one of a pair of marquetry commodes attributed to John Cobb. The glasses were acquired by Queen Mary in 1932 and the commodes by Queen Elizabeth in 1944.

me to paint her. Needless to say I am at her service and would love to do her portrait whenever it is possible.'

The Queen did not see the war as an obstacle to sitting to him, and, although John had thought of an informal portrait painted at Windsor Castle, it was finally arranged that a formal portrait to be a symbol of the Queen in wartime should be painted at Buckingham Palace.

The first sitting was fixed for 31 October, but John cancelled that, and painting only got under way the following month. Early in 1940 sittings were moved to another room. Then they were held up, because, as the Queen's private secretary reported, 'The temperature in the Yellow Room is indistinguishable to that reported in Finland.' Sittings were resumed in March. In June 1940, John wrote to Mrs Cazalet: 'She has been absolutely angelic in posing so often and with such cheerfulness.' However, as Michael Holroyd has written, John was overcome by shyness and 'he could make no real contact with her – she was not real. He wanted to make her real ... Good God. It was an impossible situation.'

After that, to help him relax, sherry was introduced into the sittings. Then a bottle of brandy was put into the cupboard kept for his painting things. Next the Queen suggested some music, and the Griller Quartet was introduced into the next room to play soothing music by English composers. That, however, was a failure: first John misheard their name and thought they were the Gorilla Quartet; and then he said how could he listen to music and paint. Even so by late June 1940, John was able to write to Mrs Cazalet: 'it looks very near done to a turn'. However in the end it was the Blitz that brought the sittings to an end.

In the autumn the picture was taken to John's studio in the country where he continued to look at it: 'I can see a good Johnish picture there – *not* a Cecil Beaton creation or anything of that sort.' But, despite prodding from the Queen, he was not able to continue.

That is a great pity, because whereas almost all portraits show the Queen in repose, as if silent and still, it is as if John tried to express both his image of her as Queen and the sparkle of her personality and conversation through the sparkle of her diamonds and rubies (which he had never painted before), and the sequins in her dress, which was one of those in which Cecil Beaton had taken his first, famous, photographs of her at Buckingham Palace in 1939. While complete success eluded him in that impossible task, the way he painted her dress and jewels succeeds in capturing a reflection of her personality. When the King encouraged her

80. *The Garden Room.*

to revive the crinoline, he could not have known how successful it would be or how a dress designed by Hartnell could project her personality to many people who might not have a chance to talk to the Queen, but could only see the dress sparkling as it reflected her distinctive carriage and movements. John seems to have gone after that idea in a way not attempted by any other painter or photographer.

After 1942 the picture disappeared from sight, and it was only rediscovered in 1961 when it was exhibited at Tooths. Shortly afterwards it was presented to the Queen when she launched the passenger liner SS *Northern Star* by General Sir Charles Dunphie (chairman of Vickers Armstrong, who built the ship on Tyne-side), and by Viscount Knollys (chairman of the Shaw Savile line).

87

81. Queen Elizabeth *by Augustus John, begun 1939.*

Close by it, just to the right of the chimneypiece, is a portrait of Queen Elizabeth that is a complete contrast, not only in dress but in way of painting. It is the sketch that James Gunn painted of her on 26 November 1945, when he was working on the big portrait of her as Royal Bencher of the Middle Temple (82). The artist had been asked to paint the King in 1944 and later he painted the famous conversation piece of the King and Queen with the Princesses at Royal Lodge, which is in the National Portrait Gallery. Queen Elizabeth owns one of the large drawings for it but with a different background.

The sketch of Queen Elizabeth shows what a good painter Gunn was and how he deserved the exhibition held at the National Portrait Gallery of Scotland in 1994. The Middle Temple portrait was not available for the exhibition, but surprisingly neither this sketch nor the Montgomery picture were asked for. Gunn did not keep a diary and wrote no account of painting the Queen, which was one of his most enjoyable experiences as a portrait painter. He was clearly satisfied with the picture, because he painted a copy of the sketch for himself before he sent the first version to the Queen. He bought a special small yellow bergère for the Queen to sit in for the picture.

If those two pictures make one surprising juxtaposition in the room, there is a second on the long inner wall – *The Eve of St Agnes* by Sir John Everett Millais (1829–96) (83), which Queen Elizabeth acquired for the Collection in 1942. It was an imaginative purchase, particularly at that date, because it is the only significant Pre-Raphaelite picture in the Royal Collection, a gap that might have been filled if Prince Albert had not died in 1861. Many years later, in 1977, when the sketch for the figure of Madeline turned up in a sale, Queen Elizabeth bought it so that they could hang on the same wall at Clarence House (84).

The picture illustrates a passage in Keats's poem. Madeline

82. Queen Elizabeth, *a sketch by James Gunn.*

Loosens her fragrant boddice; by degrees
Her rich attire creeps rustling to her knees:
Half-hidden, like a mermaid in sea-weed,
Pensive awhile she dreams awake, and sees
In fancy, fair St Agnes in her bed.

According to Millais's son, his father had been struck by Keats's lines in the autumn of 1862 and came south to work on the picture in the King's Room at Knole, taking lodgings in Sevenoaks. His wife posed for the figure, and most of the picture was done in the course of three bitterly cold nights when moonlight streamed in through the window, bathing the figure in an eerie blue light and leaving the great bed of shimmering gold brocade in a brown shadow. The picture was shown at the Royal Academy in 1863.

The Millais is balanced in the eastern part of the room by a large and characteristically jolly Bassano of lots of animals and given a serious title and purpose by the presence of Noah's Ark; that was bought in 1964. On the east wall is a large portrait of Charles I after Van Dyck, bought in 1951, flanked by two portraits by Jan Mytens of the Countess de la Gardie and the Princess of Orange.

Among the furniture in the room is a fine Louis Quinze *bureau plat* stamped by

J. C. Ellaume, which had belonged to the Marquess of Lincolnshire and came from Carrington House, Whitehall. It was probably sold at Christie's in December 1928. To the right of it can be seen a pair of square-backed Italian Empire chairs that belonged to Miss Violet Cavendish-Bentinck, Queen Elizabeth's aunt.

However the most important objects are the pair of mid-18th-century Chinese mirror paintings in gilded frames that hang above a pair of commodes formerly in the collection of Pierpont Morgan (79). The latter were spotted by Sir Arthur Penn and acquired by Queen Elizabeth in 1944.

In the past the commodes have been attributed to John Cobb, but in her recent catalogue of those in the Lady Lever Collection, Lucy Wood has grouped them with a commode of much more obviously French form at Ham House and the puzzling commode from St Giles's House in the Metropolitan Museum, suggesting that they may be by one of the Swedish cabinet-makers who came to London

83. The Eve of St Agnes *by Sir John Everett Millais, 1862.*

90

via Paris in the late 1760s. Lucy Wood also makes a comparison between the marquetry sprays of flowers suspended from loops on Queen Elizabeth's commodes and the marquetry on a commode of similar shape at Nostell Priory, Yorkshire and on another, rather larger, one at Hatfield House, Hertfordshire. The tops are inlaid with vases derived from French prints that are akin to others.

The mirror paintings have particularly good decorative frames, full of fantasy and light. The inner frame holding the glass is disguised by the slender tree trunks growing up the sides, an idea that could come from Pillement's prints published in 1759, and they turn into a Chinese landscape at the top with single figures in the central pavilions.

They were bought by Queen Mary from her son-in-law, the Earl of Harewood, in March 1932, shortly before the sale of the remaining contents of Chesterfield House in London that took

84. *Millais's sketch for the figure of Madeline in* The Eve of St Agnes.

place on 7 April 1932. In her copy of that sale catalogue, Queen Mary recorded the lots that she bought, but since the glasses are not listed there, they must have been acquired privately, because she included the month of March in her immaculate catalogue of her additions to her collection.

The Morning Room

Already a visitor will have gathered a sense of the strong 20th-century representation in Queen Elizabeth's pictures, but even so no one would expect to find pictures of such quality and range as are found in this room, ranging as they do from Fantin Latour and Monet to Sickert, Augustus John and Paul Nash. If her interest owed a good deal to the encouragement of Sir Jasper Ridley and Sir Kenneth Clark, it should also be remembered that among her cousins were Lady Ottoline Morrell and Lady Ottoline's brother, Lord Henry Bentinck. Their father was a brother of Queen Elizabeth's maternal grandfather, and Queen Elizabeth's grandmother, by then Mrs Scott, was one of the first people to be kind to Lady Ottoline. Lady Ottoline was one of the founders of the Contemporary Art Society and Lord Henry was its president in succession to Philip Morrell, and both were on the committee for the Post-Impressionist exhibition in 1910. They were friends of Lady Strathmore, but sadly too old to have become friends of her daughter. Queen Elizabeth has been Patron of the Contemporary Art Society since 1947.

Whether entering the room from the Hall or the Library, it is the grouping of the pictures and objects that holds one's attention (85–7). By the doors is the group in Plate 86. On the north wall is Fantin Latour's *Azaleas and Pansies* and at right angles to it *A Fylde Farm* by L.S. Lowry, signed and dated 1943, while on the easel is one of the two drawings of Queen Elizabeth done by Sargent at the time of her marriage in 1923. It was then that Sargent said that the Queen was 'The only completely unselfconscious sitter I have ever had.'

Behind the easel is an informal stack of pictures that include some by friends and others that must be there to tease; and, contrary to appearances of casualness, they are arranged according to who is coming to see Queen Elizabeth.

Over the chimneypiece with its Louis Seize clock and candelabra and Ch'ien-lung cocks is a small bust of Sir Winston Churchill done by Reid-Dick in 1942, which the Queen saw when she was sitting to the sculptor (88). That immediately brings memories of the war into the room in a most striking and moving way, underlying the partnership of King and Prime Minister. In particular it reminds the Queen of Sir Winston's weekly visits to the Palace, sometimes hunched in gloom, and then one day saying to the King 'I bring you victory' –

85. *The Morning Room seen through the Library door.*

93

86. Left *A group of pictures in a corner of the Morning Room. On the walls hang* Azaleas and Pansies *by Fantin Latour, 1881, and* A Fylde Farm *by L. S. Lowry, 1943, and on the easel a drawing of Queen Elizabeth at the time of her marriage in 1923 by J. S. Sargent.*

87. Above *A group in the opposite corner: below* When Homer Nods *by Augustus John is* A View of Sandringham, *a print after a watercolour by the Prince of Wales; the bust of Queen Elizabeth by David Cregeen is on a stand made by David Linley, Queen Elizabeth's grandson; the bronze group is a reduced version of* Sir Winston and Lady Churchill *by Oscar Nemon, which Queen Elizabeth unveiled in the garden at Chartwell, the Churchills' house in Kent.*

88. A Lady in a Pink Ballgown, Seated with a Gentleman in Green *by Walter Sickert, painted in 1941, over the Morning Room chimneypiece, with a small bust of Sir Winston Churchill by Sir William Reid-Dick, 1942.*

he had just received a dispatch from General Alexander at El Alamein and saw it as the turning point of the war.

Small as it is, the bust makes a much stronger impression than Sickert's *A Lady in a Pink Ballgown, Seated with a Gentleman in Green* that hangs above it, painted in 1941 when Sickert's powers were failing.

96

89. Study of Rocks; Creuse, Fresselines *by Claude Monet, 1889.*

To the right of the chimneybreast hangs Monet's *Study of Rocks* (89) and at right angles to it on the window wall the Sickert *Conversation Piece at Aintree* (90). They are balanced in the southwest corner by the Augustus John of G.B. Shaw known as *When Homer Nods* (91). Below that is a print after one of the Prince of Wales's watercolours of Sandringham; a bust of Queen Elizabeth by David Cregeen, one of the three casts of the bust done for the Middle Temple, on a pedestal designed by her grandson David Linley; and to the left of that a miniature version of Oscar Nemon's group of Sir Winston and Lady Churchill, which was given to her when she unveiled the full-size statue at Chartwell, Sir Winston and Lady Churchill's house in Kent (87). (Those with sharp eyes may spot the dogs' tennis ball in the corner of the chair, which the photographer did not remove.)

In the northwest corner of the room is Nash's *Vernal Equinox* (92), and in the

90. Conversation Piece at Aintree *by Walter Sickert, after 1927.*

season of azaleas one flowers below it in a huge pot, echoing the Fantin Latour on the other side of the door.

It is natural to want to know how the pictures came together. The Fantin Latour, which was painted in 1881, was left to Queen Elizabeth by Mrs Audrey Pleydell Bouverie in 1968. The daughter of W.D. James of West Dean and first married to Marshall Field of Chicago, she had several houses including St John's Lodge, Regent's Park, and Julians in Hertfordshire, decorated with great style and filled with fine pictures, some of which she lent to an exhibition at the Tate Gallery in 1954.

Mrs Pleydell Bouverie also shared Queen Elizabeth's pleasure in Chelsea vegetables.

Monet's *Study of Rocks* was recommended to the Queen in 1945 by Sir Gerald Kelly, when he was completing painting the State Portraits, and he made a copy of it that Queen Elizabeth thought so good that she insisted he should sign it to be sure there was no confusion in the future.

The *Study of Rocks* was painted in March–April 1889, when Monet (1840–1926) returned to the village of Fresselines, in the middle of France, to paint the setting of the river Creuse. After not sending anything in to the fifth Impressionist exhibition in 1880, the painter became increasingly independent. He established his family at Giverny in 1883, and then made long expeditions to a series of places where he concentrated on painting variations on a few landscape themes, a pattern of work that preceded his series of grain stacks, poplars and Rouen Cathedral in the 1890s. Having been taken to Fresselines in February 1889, he decided to return to paint its winter landscape. On 31 March he wrote:

By looking very hard I finally entered into the spirit of this countryside, I understand it now and have a clearer idea of what to do with it.

The artist gave the *Study of Rocks* to Georges Clemenceau in 1899.

At right angles to it hangs *A Conversation Piece at Aintree* by Sickert (1860–1942) which shows King George V and his stud manager Major F. H. W. Fetherstonhaugh. It was based on a photograph of the two men seen through a car window that appeared in the *News Chronicle* on 25 March 1927. Sickert made extensive use of photographs in this way, basing two other royal pictures on them, but such paintings were not considered 'cricket'. This picture was rejected by the Glasgow Art Gallery in 1931 as not being majestic enough; then by the Tate Gallery; by the Victoria Art Gallery at Bath and by King George VI and Queen Elizabeth in 1939. It was finally bought by Her Majesty in 1951.

Sickert, on one side of the big window, is balanced by John, with his third portrait of Bernard Shaw called *When Homer Nods*, painted when both were staying with Lady Gregory at Coole Park in the

91. When Homer Nods, *a portrait of G. B. Shaw by Augustus John, 1915.*

west of Ireland in 1915. Lady Gregory had first invited Augustus John to Coole Park in 1907 to paint W. B. Yeats at the suggestion of her son, Robert, whose best man John had been. Shaw and his wife stayed with her again for Easter in 1915, and in 1920 Lady Gregory wrote an account of what had happened on that occasion:

... in talking one evening with him and Mrs Shaw, I found there had never been a good portrait painted of him. We called out that it must be done, but he said that he had no

92. Vernal Equinox *by Paul Nash*.

time for sittings. He agreed that if he were to sit, John was the artist he would choose
... Next day I telegraphed to John and in a few days he arrived. He made the two portraits that GBS possesses and then he went on to another. I went to the studio when
this was going on and John made me a sign not to speak, and I saw that his sitter, tired
at last, had fallen asleep.

Of the portraits Shaw owned two, but one he gave to the Fitzwilliam Museum at Cambridge; the other remains in his house at Ayot St Lawrence. Queen Elizabeth's picture was bought by an Australian, who later sold it in London, and she acquired it in 1938.

Facing the John at the north end of the room is the most poetic picture in the house, *Vernal Equinox*, by Paul Nash (1889–1946) which Queen Elizabeth bought in 1943 at the suggestion of Sir Jasper Ridley. A little later the artist wrote to his friend and fellow painter, Edward Burra:

... Did I tell you I have sold a picture to the Queen or rather she has purchased one from Toothypegs. She won't admit it apparently (T saw a reproduction in the Times & all that) May be she's ashamed of her violent act. I'm about to commit myself on a large scale again. Nightpiece of the aerial invasion of Hunland. Same size as the Battle of Britain ...

Fortunately we have the artist's own explanation for the picture:

All my recent landscapes are, as it were, recreations of an actual scene – the prospect as seen from the house I go to stay at on Boar's Hill where there is a wide window ... looking across the garden to the Berkshire Downs on the horizon. Between the farthest woods and the downs rise up the twin hills of the Wittenham Clumps ... Actually they are a long way from Boar's Hill and I have to look at them through my field glasses to get an adequate view of them ...

Call it, if you like, a transcendental conception; a landscape of the imagination which has evolved in two ways: on the one hand through a personal interpretation of the phenomenon of the equinox, on the other through the inspiration derived from an actual place. In each so-called truths of knowledge and appearance have been disregarded where it seemed necessary.

Either side of the chimneypiece are alcoves filled with Chelsea china of which Queen Elizabeth has formed a considerable collection, as will be explained in the description of her Sitting Room on page 139.

The Library

This is not a library in the full sense of a room to settle down and read in or make into a base for daily life, having been originally formed by Nash as the entrance hall and only fitted up as a library for Princess Elizabeth and the Duke of Edinburgh. Queen Elizabeth wanted to create the idea of an *enfilade* from the Morning Room to the Dining Room, and so now the room has three doors on three walls and no chimneypiece. However it is always very agreeable to eat in a book room, and, since Queen Elizabeth likes the French habit of eating in different rooms, it comes into its own when it is used for lunch, as is shown here (93).

On the north wall the shelves of books are varied with objects that form a pattern. Among them are the Greek vase and figures of huntsmen in Sèvres biscuit, copies of 18th-century originals given to the Duke and Duchess of York in 1923. Sometimes the set is used on the table in the Dining Room, as can be seen in Plate 94.

The Dining Room

The Dining Room has been in this position since William IV's day, but he would not recognize the room nor the portraits. Originally it was simply treated, as can be seen from the watercolour of 1861 (13). It seems that its decoration in the Adam style was carried out for the Duke of Connaught soon after 1900, round a set of portraits of George III and his family by a follower of Beechey.

This room can be rather gloomy since it only gets sunlight on a very bright day because of the unneighbourly bulk of Lancaster House that rose in front of it as soon as the Duke of Clarence had completed his alteration. This encourages Queen Elizabeth to have a table set up in the Library, the Morning Room or the Garden Room. However at night the Dining Room can be brought to life for a dinner party with flowers and plate, as can be seen in Plates 94–6 which show the room as it would be laid for a special occasion.

Her Majesty sits in the

93. Left *The Library, arranged for lunch, with the doors open to the Dining Room.*
94. Right *A view across the table to the chimneypiece. On the table can be seen the candelabra of about 1870, sauce tureens after a design by J. J. Boileau, Sèvres huntsmen, and the trochus shell stands by Leslie Durbin.*

103

95. Above *Plate on the sideboard: between candelabra of about 1870 are a racing trophy of 1820, a 17th-century royal alms dish, with, in front, William III's helmet ewer by Garthorne and the Bowes ewer by David Willaume with faïence vegetables.*
96. Right *The Dining Room with the table laid for dinner.*

only armchair in the middle of the east side of the table with her back to the chimneypiece. A Strathmore sugar caster made by Edward Penman, an Edinburgh silversmith working at the end of the 17th century, a gold box given to her by the Fishmongers' Company in 1970, and a notepad are the only special marks of her place.

The white, yellow and pink of the flowers are echoed in the white biscuit Sèvres huntsmen with the arms of the Duke and Duchess of York that are dated 1923, and by the silver gilt (94–6). The pair of candelabra were made about 1870 and have the monogram of King Edward VII when Prince of Wales. The four sauce tureens with a royal crest on the covers are after designs by J.J. Boileau, three of which were made by Digby Scott and Benjamin Smith in 1802 with a fourth by Rundell. The trochus shells are by Leslie Durbin.

On the sideboard (95) are more pieces of silver gilt grouped round a 17th-century alms dish with the Royal Crown decorated with later trophies of arms and the labours of Hercules, and the ewer in the form of a helmet made for William III by Garthorne (133). To the left is a racing trophy made by William Bateman in 1820, which was acquired in 1949, and on the right the great ewer made by David Willaume that goes with the sideboard dish (52, 53), which is usually set out on a round table at the other end of the room. There are two more of the candelabra. Grouped with the plate are a number of faïence vegetables that make surprising but effective companions for the silver gilt, their cheerful colours and glazes 'degranding' the plate in an enjoyable way.

The total effect has a sparkle to it that would have an enlivening effect on any conversation in the room.

97. Queen Elizabeth *by Graham Sutherland, a sketch for a portrait begun in 1961 and then abandoned. The sketch was completed in 1967.*

The Stairs

Nash's staircase, which consisted of two parallel flights with a cast-iron balustrade, was curiously bleak so Queen Elizabeth replaced it with a bolder wooden staircase. The balusters have a strong early Georgian profile and end in bold scrolls and with lions on the newels. The staircase now starts with three steps at right angles to the Hall and then turns (98).

At the second turn is another of the changes of mood that are so characteristic of the house: historical portraits step unexpectedly into the second half of the 20th century with the portrait of Queen Elizabeth painted by Graham Sutherland (1903–80) (97). Sutherland had only recently begun to paint portraits when

in July 1951 the Queen saw his portrait of Somerset Maugham at the Tate Gallery. It so impressed her that she suggested that he might paint her. Nothing happened immediately, partly because of the death of the King, but the idea was not forgotten, and attempts were made to revive it in 1952, 1953 and 1954, when the artist decided he would like to paint her in a hat, because it 'added to the impression of Queenliness'. Then again there was another long pause until 1960 when London University, of which Her Majesty had been Chancellor since 1955, wanted to have a portrait of her and it was agreed that Sutherland should do it. Queen Elizabeth suggested it should be in Garter robes but the artist did not feel that was his style; then she suggested a tiara and white dress; but finally she agreed to his initial idea of painting her wearing a feathered hat. The first sitting was held on 22 March 1961, and five more were held the following week; but as Roger Berthoud has written, 'Graham eventually reached the conclusion that he would not be able to produce the sort of pic-

99. Edith and Caspar *by Augustus John, 1911.*

ture that the university wanted to hang at Senate House.' So, alas, the picture was abandoned after this sketch, which he finally completed in April 1967 and then offered to the Queen. His failure is to be regretted, because the sketch gives a sense of rapport between sitter and artist and, while never likely to be a popular picture of her, it is perhaps the liveliest ever painted.

In an article about portraits of Queen Elizabeth in 1990 Roy Strong wrote: 'Sutherland focuses on what his predecessors omitted, the acute intelligence of the sitter beneath the beguiling humour. The typically upright posture, the pensive leaning movement of the right arm, the alert turn of the head and eyes together

98. Left *Early portraits on the first flight of the stairs.*

100. Ennui *by Walter Sickert, probably about 1913.*

with the determined set of the lips penetrate the character deeply.'

Sutherland suggests her expression of interest and concentration in conversation and her sparkling sense of amusement.

After the failure of that commission, in 1963 London University asked Pietro Annigoni to paint their Chancellor, but it was no happier with the result. Among other things it had not wanted Queen Elizabeth to wear her mortar board, but Annigoni recorded: 'But she said to me, "Why shouldn't I put it on my head?", and answered her own question by doing just that.'

The Queen looks past a Louis Quinze clock-on-bracket and a sanguine drawing of *Ida Nettleship and Dorelia* by Augustus John, hanging over a little watercolour *Head of a Boy* by Sickert, to a group of 20th-century pictures: *Edith and Caspar, Dorset Study* by John, painted in 1911 (99), then a Sisley landscape, which the Queen bought in 1939, and a version of Sickert's *Ennui* (100). At the top is a painting of *The Scuola and Chiesa San Rocco* in Venice painted in 1962 by John Piper in a manner quite different from the Windsor drawings, with the architecture almost dissolving. Here there is another drawing by John, which was left to Queen Elizabeth by Mrs Cazalet.

In 1911–13 Sickert painted a long series of two-figure domestic subjects, and Wendy Baron suggests that Queen Elizabeth's picture is probably a preliminary version painted about 1913 for the larger and more highly finished picture exhibited in 1914 that is now in the Tate Gallery.

At the turn of the stairs there is a first view of the Corridor, a reversal of that below. It is lit at both ends, from above at the north end, and by a large

101. Right The Presentation of King Louis-Philippe's Grandsons to Queen Victoria at the Château d'Eu in Normandy in September 1845 *by F.X. Winterhalter.*

window framed by a tapestry lambrequin with Solomonic columns at the south end (102).

A glance up the stairs to the second storey reveals F.X. Winterhalter's picture commemorating Queen Victoria's second brief visit to King Louis-Philippe at the Château d'Eu in Normandy in 1845, when she stayed for a night in September, on the way back from Coburg (101). The artist (1806–73) had become a painter of royalty in 1838 when he painted the Queen of the Belgians and her son. That Queen had introduced him to her father, King Louis-Philippe, and arranged his first visit to the English court in 1842. Thus as well as painting state portraits of the King and Queen of the French, Winterhalter had also recorded their reception at Windsor in 1844. That is how the present picture came to be commissioned by the King of the French. In September 1845, the Queen of the Belgians wrote to Queen Victoria, her niece by marriage: 'I don't know if you know that Winterhalter is painting a picture *de la présentation* of my Father's grandsons to you. They say it is delightful.' The following month she wrote again to say that the picture had not been begun but the sketches were delightful.

The figures are set in the projected Galerie Victoria at Eu in which the King planned to hang thirty specially commissioned paintings recording Queen Victoria's first visit in 1843 and his own to Windsor, a scheme that was not complete by 1848 when he had to flee. The picture shows the King standing in the centre and wearing the Garter with Queen Victoria below him. Behind the King on the left stands the Prince of Salerno and in front of the King François, Prince de Joinville, Prince Albert and Augustus, Prince of Saxe-Coburg-Gotha. On the left sits Hélène Duchesse d'Orléans and in front of her stand her two sons, Robert, Duc de Chartres, and Louis, Comte de Paris. On the left of the Duchesse are seated the Princess of Salerno, the Duchesse d'Aumale and Madame Adélaïde. On Queen Victoria's left is seated the Queen of the French. In front of her stands Gaston, Comte d'Eu, with his brother Ferdinand, Duc d'Alençon. The boy in profile to the left, by the shoulder of the Queen of the French, is Prince Philip of Württemberg. In the foreground on the right sits Princesse Clémentine, wife of Augustus, Prince of Saxe-Coburg with her sons, Philip and Augustus, the baby in her arms.

The picture was sold at Sotheby's in 1947 and bought for the Queen.

The Corridor

The Corridor, like the Horse Corridor, is articulated by pairs of full-length portraits on the west wall and pairs of arches and spectacular Rococo glasses on the east wall. The eye is led towards the light by the strong blue upholstery on a fine set of late-18th-century settees and chairs from Preston Hall, Midlothian (110, 39). Those elements give the Corridor its sense of structure, but, since the Queen's own rooms open off it, it is arranged more informally than the Hall. Here are recent gifts of small pictures like a view of the Castle of Mey by Derek Hill, propped up on the dado rail, and cabinets of precious small objects, Fabergé, jades and Chinese snuff bottles.

102. *A southward view of the Corridor on the first floor.*

103. *A cabinet containing work by Fabergé.*

By the Drawing Room door is a dark glazed cabinet that it would be easy to pass, but when it is illuminated the world of Fabergé is revealed (103). Queen Elizabeth, like Queen Mary and Queen Alexandra before her, has long appreciated the skill, the sparkle and the fantasy of his work, but she has never sought the most extravagant fantasies produced at Easter time for the Russian Imperial family nor the hard stone animals that appealed so much to Queen Alexandra.

Instead she has collected little frames for clocks and miniatures, boxes and sprays of flowers, including one of cornflowers (104).

That, most unexpectedly, brings back the war years, as can be gathered from extracts from two letters of Queen Elizabeth to Queen Mary in 1944. On 8 July Queen Elizabeth wrote: 'It is too kind of you to say that I may find a present. The other day I found a pretty Fabergé cornflower in a crystal pot, so charming in these grim and grey days that I thought it would look cheerful in my shelter room at B. Palace. If you would care to give a little towards it, I would love that.' On 4 August Queen Elizabeth wrote again: 'It was so kind of you to take a share in the Fabergé flower, and I send you most loving thanks for a lovely present. It is a charming thing, and so beautifully unwarlike.'

The pictures start with arguably the most successful early portrait of Queen Elizabeth, the delicate but strong watercolour painted by Savely Sorine (1887–1953) at White Lodge at the time of her marriage in 1923 (106). The Russian artist was born in 1887 and studied at the Academy of Fine Arts in St Petersburg, where he won the Prix de Rome. In 1923 he was at the outset of his career in the West,

104. Above *A cornflower and oats in a crystal pot by Fabergé.*

105. Below *A presentation box of three-colour gold, yellow guilloché enamel and rose diamonds, which form on the hinged cover the crowned cypher of Tsar Nicholas II. Mark of August Frederick Hollming, 1896–1908.*

106. Queen Elizabeth at the Time of her Marriage in 1923 *by Savely Sorine (1887–1953).*

having shown for the first time at the Salon d'Automne in Paris the previous year. He was known to Prince Paul of Yugoslavia, who that same year married Princess Olga of Greece. (Her younger sister, Princess Marina, later married the Duke of Kent.) It was the Prince who introduced him to the Duke and Duchess of York.

Facing it is William Nicholson's *Gold Jug* (107). All his life Nicholson (1872–1949) enjoyed painting still lifes and in the late 1930s he painted a small series of pictures exploring light on plate: *Gold Jug* dating from 1937, *Silver* in the Tate Gallery from the following year, and *Tall Pewter Jug* from 1939. The texture of his paint had become increasingly free over the years, and one of the delights of this picture, which is hard to judge in a reproduction, is the way it is painted.

Shortly before Nicholson's 70th birthday, the first retrospective exhibition was held in London at the National Gallery. It opened on 1 January 1942, and later the same year Queen Elizabeth bought the picture directly from the artist on the recommendation of Sir Kenneth Clark. It appears to be in its original frame that has the character of being professionally made, but touched up by the artist to suit the picture.

The picture was a natural one for the Queen to choose, given her pleasure in plate, particularly silver gilt, which has already been shown in the Dining Room and which we will touch on again at the end of the book. The way Nicholson catches the play of light on the jug and the way it stands out from the background of his drawings parallels Queen Elizabeth's own delight in the different ways the play of light is handled by silversmiths, past and present, and helps to explain why tables for meals at Clarence House are to some extent ever-changing still lifes and therefore to be enjoyed in that way.

Beyond the Sorine on the east wall is the first of the Rococo glasses over 19th-century Boulle cabinets (108, 109). The glasses read as being reframings of two older pairs of plates and the carver has created a rich, if rather dense and tight effect, that is not easy to date or to place. Could it be that he was working out of London in the 1750s and still not wholly at ease with prints after Lock's drawings? It is tantalizing that they have no provenance. On the cabinet stands a bust of Queen Elizabeth as Lady Elizabeth Bowes-Lyon by Frederick Louis Roslyn (b.1878). Tucked in beside it is a Florentine bust.

The second glass is flanked by oil sketches of King George VI by Francis Hodge (1883–1949) painted in 1938–9 for

107. Gold Jug *by Sir William Nicholson, 1937.*

the portrait in admiral's uniform for the Royal College of Surgeons, and exhibited at the Royal Academy in 1939; and of King George V by Charles Sims (1873–1928) (109). The latter is a study for a full-length picture that Charles Sims painted for the Council Room of the Royal Academy when he was Keeper, because the President, Sir Aston Webb (who should have done it), was an architect. Sims's compositional sketch was well received in 1923 and the finished picture was shown at the Royal Academy in 1924. However there were doubts about it and the Academy Council got cold feet, and, as Sims explained in his book *Picture Making Technique and Inspiration* in 1934, after Sir Frank Dicksee took over from Aston Webb, the former went to see the King and afterwards he informed: 'the Keeper that his portrait was giving offence. The Keeper settled the dispute forthwith by committing it, via America, to the bonfire.' Queen Elizabeth bought the sketch for the head in 1941.

108. *One of a pair of Rococo glasses with a small Florentine bust and a bust of Lady Elizabeth Bowes-Lyon by F.L. Roslyn.*

Round the bust of Princess Victoria done by William Behnes (1795–1864) on the cabinet are watercolours commemorating picnics with Queen Elizabeth on Holkham Beach by Sir Hugh Casson.

On the facing wall is Simon Elwes's striking portrait of the King when Duke of York as Colonel of 11th Hussars, which was exhibited at the Royal Academy in 1936. The Officers of the Regiment gave it to Queen Elizabeth in his memory and to mark thirty-two years of his Colonelcy (110). To the right of it hangs a compositional study by James Gunn for what became his famous *Conversation Picture of the King and Queen with the Princesses in the Drawing Room* at Royal Lodge. That is now in the National Portrait Gallery, but here the figures are drawn in a different room.

To the left hangs *Jugs and Apples* by Matthew Smith (1861–1951), which was bought in 1940.

Among the English furniture, the outstanding element is the set of sofas and twelve armchairs from the drawing room at Preston Hall, Midlothian, which Queen Elizabeth bought at Christie's in 1947 (110, 39). Preston Hall is one of the most elegant late-18th-century houses in Scotland. Designed by Robert Mitchell, it was started in 1791 by Alexander Callender, an Indian nabob, but he died the following year. Building was continued by his brother Sir John Callender, who eventually completed it about 1800

109. *The second glass with oil sketches of King George VI by Francis Hodge, 1938–9, and of King George V by Charles Sims, 1923, and a bust of Princess Victoria by William Behnes.*

and furnished it. Sadly all Sir John's papers have disappeared. Nor does there appear to be any photograph that shows the drawing room intact with its furniture.

In a way it is odd that the set was ordered by Sir John rather than Alexander, for it has an almost Indian flavour about it that recalls the taste of Warren Hastings. But where was it made? It would have been quite usual for a Scottish owner to have gone to a London cabinet-maker. But there were also skilled chair-makers in Edinburgh in the late 18th century, as can be seen at Inveraray Castle. However the different panels of verre eglomisé, set in the backs with small pieces at the head of the legs, cannot be paralleled in any other set of chairs. It may be relevant that Francis Bamford illustrated in his pioneer survey of Scottish Cabinet Makers in *Furniture History* Vol. XIX for 1983 a pair of early 19th-century glasses with unusually extensive verre eglomisé decoration, that have the label of John Marnoch of Edinburgh. So could this set have been ordered in Edinburgh from a chair-maker in collaboration with a specialist looking-glass maker?

The set has blue satin upholstery with applied slips of earlier embroidery on them, some original but some evidently restored later by a gamekeeper's wife at Preston Hall.

In the end section beyond the door to Queen Elizabeth's Sitting Room is Mather Brown's full-length portrait of John 10th Earl of Strathmore (1764–1820) (55), flanked by *Chepstow Castle* by Wilson Steer (1860–1942) painted in 1906 (40), and a Seago.

The Steer, which was one of the first pictures bought by the Queen in 1938, is the second version of a view that he had painted in the previous year and which was accepted for the Tate Gallery as early as 1909, a decision that gave much pleasure to D. S. MacColl, who was on the staff at the time. He regarded Steer as 'our greatest landscape painter since Turner and Constable' and saw the Chepstow views as tributes to Turner, with his plate in the *Liber Studiorum* as its inspiration.

On the facing wall is a full-length portrait of Charles II by Simon Verelst (1644–1710) flanked by two paintings of St Paul's Cathedral by Duncan Grant, one bought in 1939 and the other in 1947. There are also portraits of The King and Queen when Duke and Duchess of York painted by Philip de Laszlo (1869–1937) (29, 30) in 1931. The artist first painted the Duchess at the time of her marriage in 1923 for Lady Strathmore.

110. *King George VI, when Duke of York, as Colonel of the 11th Hussars by Simon Elwes, 1936.*

The Drawing Room

When Nash remodelled the house, the Drawing Room was two separate rooms but by the Duke of Edinburgh's time a wide opening had been made between the two rooms (15). Then more of the wall was cut away later and the present columns were inserted, presumably by the Duke of Connaught about 1900 (111). The fluted coves appear in the watercolour painted in 1861 (14) and so are presumably original Nash features, but the decoration of the ceilings and the doorcases are later, thought to have been added by the Duke of Edinburgh, while the plaster panelling scheme on the walls was probably done for the Duke of Connaught. Whatever the precise date of all the detail, the room has a marvellous sense of

111. *The Drawing Room, formed out of Nash's two drawing rooms with additional late-19th- and early-20th-century decoration.*

112. *The north-east corner of the Drawing Room with one of a pair of Rococo white and gold glasses, Landseer's unfinished equestrian portrait of Queen Victoria, and a bronze bust of Queen Elizabeth by Sir William Reid-Dick.*

113. Above Queen Victoria, *an unfinished equestrian portrait by Sir Edwin Landseer, about 1838.*
114. Right John Bowes *by John Jackson over the Drawing Room chimneypiece.*

115. *A red lacquer cabinet at the south end of the Drawing Room.*

calm. Like the Dining Room below, the room only gets a little reflected sunlight, but the often grey light creates a soft effect with the ivories, old whites and old golds, and the sparkle of the chandeliers and girandoles reflected in the looking-glasses. Thus it comes into its own as an evening room.

Over the years it has become more of a portrait room, as can be seen in the background to Sir William Hutchinson's portrait of Queen Elizabeth exhibited in 1968: at that time the portrait of Master John Bowes by John Jackson and the Landseer of Queen Victoria had not yet arrived, and the Wilkie of Princess Victoria was above the chimneypiece. Surely given John Bowes's strong awareness of his anomalous position in the society of his own time, he would be pleased, and amused, to find himself in such a position and in such company (114).

In the middle of the east wall is the portrait of the three daughters of Archdeacon Cavendish-Bentinck painted in 1864 by Sir William Blake Richmond (21). The Archdeacon was the grandfather of Queen Elizabeth, and the central figure in the group is his eldest daughter, who married the future Lord Strathmore in 1881. The artist (1842–1921), who was the son of George Richmond, became well known as a portrait painter in the early 1860s, going to 'country houses as a kind of itinerant artist. The portraits I made were elaborate and they took me a long time.' He specialized in children, but that could not have been easy for them.

That portrait is flanked by the sketch by Sir Edwin Landseer (1802–73) of Queen Victoria (113) and by Wilkie's

116. The Duchess of Kent and Princess Victoria *by Sir David Wilkie, about 1832.*

The Duchess of Kent and Princess Victoria (116), with three drawings for the latter beneath it.

The Landseer appears to be his earliest picture of Queen Victoria and was painted at the turn of the year 1837–8, as a first stage towards an equestrian portrait that was never completed. The Queen first commented on Landseer's pictures at the Royal Academy in 1833, when she described them as 'very fine', and she referred to him admiringly after that. However she did not meet him until 24 November 1837. By 23 January 1838, he had done some sketches that she noted as: 'intended for the picture he is to paint of me on horseback'. Lord Melbourne, however, commented: 'somehow none of these appear to me quite handy'. Progress was slow, and on 9 January 1839 the Queen and Melbourne talked of Landseer's 'idleness and laziness, not coming to Windsor when I said he might paint me, etc, which Lord M. said was wrong; then never sending in his bill'. Landseer, for his part, found the Queen demanding and in the early 1840s he described her as 'a very *inconvenient* little treasure'. This sketch remained in Landseer's possession and was sold in 1874 after his death.

On the back of the picture is pasted a typed copy of a letter from Henry Ponsonby sent from Windsor Castle to Lord Harcourt in December 1881. He wrote:

The Queen was very much interested to hear that you had bought Landseer's unfinished picture of her when young. She remembers it well and the numerous sittings she gave. On one occasion he had a horse in the room which she mounted and he painted her on it. But like many of his works, he left it unfinished and she had forgotten all about it till you have mentioned it.

Her Majesty hopes you will not think she ever wore her hat as Landseer represented it. He insisted on placing it so for artistic reasons, but much against her will.

The picture reappeared at Christie's in 1948 when it was bought by Queen Elizabeth.

Nothing appears to be known of who commissioned the picture by Wilkie or why it was left unfinished. The picture used to be called *The First Communion of Queen Victoria* (116), but, when it was exhibited at the Wilkie exhibition at the Royal Academy in 1958, it was suggested that it is more likely to commemorate the Princess's thirteenth birthday in 1832 rather than her confirmation when she was sixteen in 1835. To the right of the Princess appears her mother, the Duchess of Kent, with the Duchess's brother, Prince Leopold (later King of the Belgians), and on the left the Duchess's son by her first marriage, Prince Charles of Leiningen; the female figure behind the Duchess may be her daughter Princess Feodora; the bust on the left is of the Duke of Kent. The picture was later in the collection of the Earl of Leven and given to The Queen in 1948 by Captain Michael Wemyss.

Below it hangs a frame with three studies for the picture by Wilkie, which Queen Elizabeth bought in 1964. On the back is a label in a 19th-century hand that says 'HRH The Duchess of Kent and Queen Victoria when 12 years of age 1831'. That appears to support an even earlier date for the painting.

On the window wall is a fine Lawrence drawing of George IV that relates to the last portrait Lawrence painted of him (117). The original portrait, which shows George IV in day dress and wearing the Garter Star, was painted for the Marchioness Conyngham and is now in the Wallace Collection.

The low tones of the pictures are complemented by the furniture. Queen Elizabeth bought the pair of Rococo glasses flanking the chimneypiece that happily retain their original white and gold decoration, which is often prettier than solid gilding (112). She also acquired the over-the-top gilded glass above the chimneypiece at the south end of the room;

117. King George IV, *a drawing by Sir Thomas Lawrence c.1822.*

that combines Chinamen with rushing hounds in the manner of Lock's designs (115).

They go well with the main suite of seat furniture that comes from the Royal Collection and is revealing of Queen Elizabeth's eye, because she selected for Clarence House what has turned out to be the only set of Chippendale chairs in the Collection. The set was identified when Christopher Gilbert, who had been working on Chippendale, saw a 70th-birthday photograph of Queen Elizabeth sitting on one of the chairs in *The Sunday Times.* That led him to ask about its history, and it was established that the set bore the inventory mark of King George IV. That in turn was important because the design was not only very close to the documented Brocket Hall suite of about 1773, but it seemed to confirm Chippendale's excuse in early 1768 that he was behind with his commissions for Sir

Rowland Winn at Nostell Priory as a result of his work for the Royal Family. That excuse had been a puzzle, because no trace of his name could be found in the Lord Chamberlain's accounts. However the journal of Thomas Mowat, a Shetlander who went to London in 1775, recorded that he had met the Chippendales and had gone to Gloucester House, the residence of George III's younger brother, with the younger Chippendale and also to Windsor Castle with their partner, Thomas Haig. Since then payments to Chippendale totalling £134 15s 6d in the years 1764–7 have come to light in the bank account of the Duke of Gloucester, who came of age in 1764 and was given the title that year. They, however, are too early for the style of the suite at Clarence House and it seems unlikely that the Duke of Gloucester was ordering drawing-room furniture about 1773, because in 1772 (after the passing of the Royal Marriage Act that year) the Duke acknowledged his secret marriage in 1766 to Maria Countess Waldegrave and was banished from the Court.

The Clarence House suite now consists of two sofas, eight armchairs and five side chairs with composition ornament; but in 1866 it was considerably larger. Evidently it had been extended at some date.

By far the most colourful object in the room is the late-17th-century lacquer cabinet with unusually elaborate silver gesso carving (115). It sings out here, as it would do in any room, and it is not difficult to imagine Queen Elizabeth choosing it to enliven palace rooms. Formerly in the collection of the Marquess Curzon, it was bought by Queen Elizabeth in 1938.

Queen Elizabeth's Sitting Room

If the Drawing Room is the most formal room in the house, an evening room and about past generations, the Sitting Room catches all the midday sun. It is hung with pale blue damask that relates to the grey marble in the 18th-century chimneypiece installed by Queen Elizabeth, and so has a drawing-room character. But it is very much to do with present-day life: it is Her Majesty's working room. Not only is there a big desk, with stands for baskets and files within easy reach, but there is another writing table in front of the fire, and every space that is not for work is deep in photographs.

As in the Morning Room there is a strong sense of grouping, with small-scale sculpture playing an active role. This can be seen on the commode to the left of the chimneypiece (121) and on the sofa table at the north end of the room (124), where a bronzed plaster figure of the King in Garter robes by Reid-Dick and a biscuit figure of the Great Duke of Wellington are seen below Terence Cuneo's sketch of the *Crowning of The Queen* in 1953.

Among the other portraits in the room is one of Sir Gerald Kelly's sketches of King George VI for the State Portrait painted at Windsor Castle, but not with the final background of a miniature set based on Viceroy's House in Delhi that Sir Edwin Lutyens designed for Kelly (123). Queen Elizabeth bought it in 1980, one of the many fruit of an amazingly long drawn-out saga. In 1938 Sir Kenneth Clark had suggested that Kelly should be commissioned to paint

118. The Madonna and Child *attributed to Zanobi Strozzi or the Master of the Buckingham Palace Madonna, about 1450. It was bought for the Royal Collection by the Prince Consort.*

131

the State Portraits of the King and Queen as 'the most reliable portrait painter of his time'. Nine feet by six feet, they were intended for the private apartments at Windsor Castle and for widespread copying for official buildings in the long-established tradition. In October 1939, the huge pictures (by then nearly complete) were moved for safety from Kelly's studio in Gloucester Place in London to Windsor Castle. There Kelly spent the whole of the war trying to finish them, which he finally did in time for the Royal Academy in 1945. He may have strained his

119. Left *In Queen Elizabeth's Sitting Room.*
120. Right *A Louis Seize clock by Kinable with enamel decoration by Coteau.*
121. Below *Busts and photographs on a commode.*

welcome at Windsor, but he worked exceedingly hard at them under what must have been difficult conditions, taking immense pains over all the details of the settings and the regalia. Like Gunn, Kelly is an artist in need of a more sympathetic view and he could rise to the particular demands of State Portraits. No doubt in the future they will be admired, but, in fact, they were not copied as was the intention and were only reproduced as black-and-white prints.

The whole story of the commission is

122. Above *An unfinished portrait of Queen Elizabeth by Sir Gerald Kelly, about 1938, painted when he was beginning the State Portraits.*
123. Right *A sketch for the State Portrait of King George VI by Sir Gerald Kelly.*
124. Opposite The Crowning of the Queen, *a sketch made at the Coronation in 1953 by Terence Cuneo, and a bronzed plaster figure of King George VI in Garter robes by Sir William Reid-Dick.*

125. Left *A late-18th-century cabinet in the manner of Ince and Mayhew. Queen Elizabeth acquired it in 1947 to display Chelsea porcelain.*
126. Top right *A large Chelsea lobed botanical plate painted with figs, asparagus, nuts and turnips.*
127. Bottom right *A group of Chelsea vegetables with an oval dish.*

given in Derek Hudson's *For Love of Painting. The Life of Sir Gerald Kelly* that he wrote in 1975, three years after Kelly's death. Kelly found:

The King didn't like wearing his coronation clothes. He dressed well and wore his everyday suits with ease and distinction, and I was told that uniform presented no problems for him; but I think it might be said of the coronation costume that it was almost a stage garment, it wasn't really a uniform ... He put these on, but he was self-conscious and uncomfortable. I had to try to solve the problem of persuading this modest man to strike some decorative pose, because I had got it firmly into my head that a State Portrait should be romantically decorative. The King was infinitely patient. He didn't like posing and he didn't pose for long, but he did pose frequently.

The Queen, however:

... was a different story. It is hard to suggest the admiration and affection which grew all around her. From wherever one looked at her, she looked nice: her face, her voice, her smile, her skin, her colouring – everything was right.

While there are many studies of the King (and some in Garter robes, possibly

137

relating to the King's unfulfilled commission given in 1941 to paint him as Sovereign of the Order of the Garter), there are even more pictures of the Queen (122). It is interesting to see that the early ones seem to anticipate Cecil Beaton's more famous photographs taken in 1939. Queen Elizabeth has one of the unfinished portraits of herself in the room.

In the corner of the room looking down on her desk is the *Madonna and Child* ascribed to Zanobi Strozzi or the Master of the Buckingham Palace Madonna that appears as a talisman for Queen Elizabeth (118). It was bought by the Prince Consort and is one of the few pictures from the Royal Collection in the house.

On the chimneypiece is one of the prettiest clocks in the house, made by Kinable in Paris, who worked between 1780 and 1825, with enamel work by Coteau who was a well-known specialist in the late 18th century (120).

Facing the chimneypiece is a particularly elegant late-18th-century cabinet with marquetry decoration in the manner of Ince and Mayhew (125). It was bought by the Queen in 1947 at the time when she was collecting Chelsea. The cabinet now contains a garden of fruit and vegetables as well as botanical plates (126–9). The lettuce tureen in the centre of Plate 127, for instance, and the pair of asparagus tureens that flank it were bought in 1947 and the pair of cauliflowers in 1949, while the pair of cabbage bowls were a Christmas present from the King in 1948. The melons in Plate 129 were bought in 1946 and the apple in 1947. However Queen Elizabeth's first pieces of Chelsea were a pair of sunflower plates, acquired in 1937. One of them is shown in Plate 129. She has concentrated on botanical plates produced in the 1750s, finding some examples decorated after the plates drawn by Ehret for his brother-in-law, Philip Miller, curator of the Chelsea Physic garden, for his *Gardener's Dictionary* of 1752 and *Figures of the most Beautiful, Useful and Uncommon Plants described in the Gardener's Dictionary* of 1755–6.

128. Above left *A large Chelsea botanical dish painted with convolvulus and butterflies.*
129. Bottom left *A group of Chelsea fruit with one of a pair of sunflower plates.*

The Plate Room

The Plate Room of a great country house is always an intriguing idea, but, alas, all too often now the best things have gone, leaving only a few good objects and a melancholy sense of little traffic to and from the dining room. However to watch a trolley-load of plate being trundled in and then see a knowledgeable butler start to lay a table and sidetables is an exciting experience, as if one is taking part in setting a stage for a performance.

At Clarence House that sense of anticipation starts in the Plate Room where three sides of the room are lined with illuminated glazed cupboards containing sparkling silver and silver gilt. It is a brave sight, even if hard to digest at first. Only a specialist would be able to spot the more interesting pieces or sense that some, like Wakelin's salad dishes, do not show their faces while others hide, like the 3rd Earl of Strathmore's rosewater dish of 1684 which is behind a silver cow (131). However when pieces are taken out and placed on the baize-covered cabinet in the centre of the room, an evocative history of plate collecting unfolds.

Queen Elizabeth's plate could be said to start with the wedding presents that she and the Duke of York received in 1923 (130). Among them was a silver cup made by Digby Scott and Benjamin Smith in 1805 that was given by the City of Westminster, and a pair of neo-classical wine coolers made by Paul Storr in 1809–10 that were given by Australia.

At that stage, however, there were no significant purchases. They only started in 1937, with the little German *setzbecher* made in Nuremberg about 1600 with the mark WG. Thereafter the purchases continued for about twenty-five years. They were mainly plate for the Dining Room, with a great deal of silver gilt of the Regency period for use on formal occasions. There is a small group of pieces with Strathmore or Bowes histories, as we have seen (47, 48, 52, 54), and a much larger one of pieces that have belonged to earlier members of the Royal Family, including several from the collections of the Dukes of Sussex and York which have been bought back by Queen Elizabeth (135).

In addition there are many presentations to Queen Elizabeth to commemorate

130. *The Plate Room. In the centre is a silver cup by Digby Scott and Benjamin Smith dated 1805, a pair of neo-classical wine coolers by Paul Storr dated 1809–10, and two vegetable dishes made in Paris by Henri Auguste for the Duke of York in 1788–9.*

visits or events or her associations with the Services. These range from the 16th-century German casket (3), which was given to her when she launched the *Queen Elizabeth* at John Brown's shipyard in 1938, to the trochus shells (5) made by Leslie Durbin that commemorate her opening of the Kariba Dam in 1960. Finally there is a group of her own racing trophies (132).

Where the plate is unusual, and possibly unique, is that it is not a collection in the modern sense of examples of the work of particular makers or chosen to show the development of forms or styles: it is primarily for use, to make a splendid show in the Dining Room and to add to the sparkle of a dinner party.

The earliest piece with a royal history is a silver-gilt wine cup dated 1660 with the crown and monogram of William and Mary. There is also a large silver-gilt

131. *A group of figurative silver mainly relating to regiments with which Queen Elizabeth has had close associations.*

132. Above *Some of Queen Elizabeth's race cups.*

133. Below left *A silver-gilt ewer in the form of a helmet with the crown and monogram of King William* III *and Queen Mary by George Garthorne, 1690.*

134. Below right *Circular and fan-shaped silver-gilt dishes with the arms of King George* I *from the diplomatic plate of Sir Paul Methuen by Louis Mettayer, 1714.*

communion cup with the arms and monogram of William III that was made by
George Garthorne in 1697. However a
slightly earlier piece by Garthorne is illustrated here: a silver-gilt ewer in the shape
of a helmet that was made in 1690 and
which has the crown and monogram of
William and Mary (133). The unusual
helmet shape suggests the continuing interest in Mannerist forms in plate that continued into the time of William Kent, but
could it also be an early example of his-
toricism in plate that parallels some of the
early castle-style restorations and re-
modellings of the time? The body of the
vessel is decorated with three trophies and
dragons in relief.

If the Garthorne ewer stands for the
English response to Huguenot forms,
Huguenot makers are represented by a
group of four circular and four fan-shaped
silver-gilt dishes (134) with the simplest
decoration. These were made in 1714 by

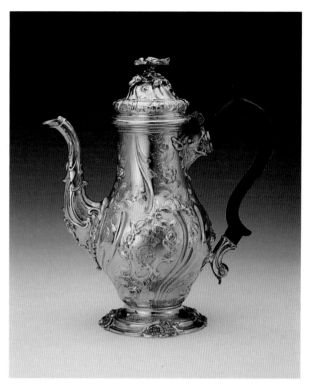

136. *A silver-gilt coffee pot by Jonathan Swift, about
1745, with the later arms of King George IV when Prince
of Wales.*

Louis Mettayer, who came from Poitou and was apprenticed to David Willaume,
the maker of the great sideboard dish and ewer. These dishes, bearing the arms
of George I, were part of the diplomatic plate supplied to Sir Paul Methuen when
he was appointed Ambassador to Spain and Morocco. He is now mainly remembered for the collection of pictures that led his heir to build the great gallery at
Corsham Court in Wiltshire. More of the dishes are in the Royal Collection, and
others are part of the Untermyer gift to the Metropolitan Museum in New York.

While the Mettayer dishes belonged to King George I, a number of Queen
Elizabeth's royal acquisitions have belonged to later royal collectors of plate and
have that as an additional point. Among the collectors was Prince Augustus

135. *A silver-gilt cup by Augustine Courtauld, 1738, with the initials and arms of Prince
Augustus Frederick, Duke of Sussex, third son of King George III.*

145

137. One of a pair of silver-gilt dishes by Samuel Wakelin, 1750, with the later arms of King George IV when Prince of Wales, possibly added in 1812.

Frederick, the third son of King George III, who was created Duke of Sussex in 1801. Like several of his brothers, he had difficulties with his father over his marriage, because in 1793 he made a clandestine marriage with Lady Augusta Murray, a Roman Catholic. The marriage was declared void by the King in 1794. However the couple weathered the storm, spending several years in Italy in the 1790s. The Prince was known as a supporter of liberal and intellectual causes, supporting the abolition of slavery, the emancipation of Catholics and the repeal of the Corn Laws. He was President of the Society of Arts in 1816 and of the Royal Society in 1830. Not only did he build up a great library at Kensington Palace, but he was also a great patron of silversmiths. Thus the sale of his plate after his death in 1843 and that of the Duke of York in 1827 were among the saleroom sensations of the 19th century.

It is Prince Augustus Frederick's initials and coronet that appear on the remarkable silver-gilt cup made by Augustine Courtauld in 1738 (135). It has applied and chased fruiting vine

138. Above *A set of two silver tea caddies and a sugar bowl, possibly by John Swift, 1751 and 1758, with their original box covered with tortoiseshell and with silver mounts.*

139. Below *A set of three silver-gilt chinoiserie caddies by William Cripps, 1751.*

140. *A silver-gilt salver given to Queen Charlotte by her four daughters, whose monograms appear together with the Crown, Royal Crests and Garter motto, by Storey and Elliott, 1811.*

decoration with twisted serpent handles that brilliantly exploit the contrast in textures of the matt ground and the burnished grapes. While not based on any known Kent design, there is a certain affinity to designs by Kent in Vardy's *Some Designs of Inigo Jones and William Kent*, published in 1744, in particular the stone vase at Houghton. It would be interesting to know who ordered the cup and what lies behind its distinctive decoration. It was acquired in 1947.

Some of the Rococo silver at Clarence House has similar later royal histories. The coffee pot made by Jonathan Swift about 1745 (136) has the arms of King George IV when Prince of Wales and also the arms of the Duke of Cumberland, who became King of Hanover. Like so many English Rococo creations, the shape is classical (in this case a conventional pear shape), but it is made to look Rococo through its ornament and the way that is applied: the whole body is given an appearance of twist by the curves of the flutes, by the sprays of flowers in relief, and the angle of the cartouche. It was acquired in 1950.

Similarly the silver-gilt dishes made by Samuel Wakelin in 1750 (137) later belonged to King George IV when Prince of Wales. He had his arms splendidly engraved on them and also ordered a matching pair from Robert Garrard in 1812. Between the swirling flutes are panels of cast decoration composed of tiny shells in two patterns alternating round the dish, with two slightly different panels found on the undersides of the dish.

148

Queen Elizabeth's enjoyment of chinoiserie objects can be seen in a set of three silver-gilt tea caddies by William Cripps of 1751 (139). Each one has a pair of slightly different scenes of figures and landscapes and a pair of cartouches.

Another set of a pair of silver caddies with covered sugar bowl (138), possibly by John Swift and made in 1751 and 1758, still has its beautifully shaped tortoiseshell box with silver mounts.

While the pieces of Rococo silver acquired by the royal princes express one aspect of their taste, it is interesting to see at Clarence House the converse of that: their liking for up-to-date French design that was the equivalent of Henry Holland's interiors of

141. *A pair of chinoiserie silver candlesticks made by Edward Farrell, 1821.*

the 1780s. That liking can be seen in the pair of silver vegetable dishes made by Henri Auguste in Paris in 1788–9 for the Duke of York, whose arms they bear (130). Henri Auguste took over from his father in 1785 and, having become *orfèvre du roi*, he lightened and made more elegant the neo-classical style of his father. These dishes probably relate to the set of twelve three-light candelabra made for the Duke of York in 1789, of which two are in the Metropolitan Museum.

One of the most elegant pieces of Regency plate is the silver-gilt salver given to Queen Charlotte by her four daughters (140). It has the Crown, Royal Crests and Garter motto and also the monograms of Princesses Elizabeth, Augusta, Mary

and Sophia. It was made by Storey and Elliott in 1811. The plain centre that shows off the engraving so well is encircled with basket work with an outer border of vine leaves and grapes.

The selection of pieces illustrated here ends with a pair of splendid chinoiserie candlesticks by Edward Farrell (1779/81?–1850) dated 1821 (141). Here Queen Elizabeth's fondness for chinoiserie objects is combined with a royal association, for they bear the Royal Arms that are puzzling for the date: Mr Arthur Grimwade has suggested that they must have been commissioned before King George III died in January 1820, and were made before King George IV was crowned in July 1821.

The stems and sockets are cast from or copied closely from a candlestick by Phillips Garden dated 1756, but with a new base. However, the story may be more complicated than that because there is a set of candlesticks of a similar design at Burghley House: four made by John Crouch in 1812 and two by Edward Farrell in 1816.

Epilogue

In making a record of any important house there is always the problem of when to stop, how to include aspects that do not seem remarkable now but will interest posterity, and how to provide a record without overstepping the boundaries of privacy. With a royal house the challenge and the constraints are both greater; and what adds to that at Clarence House is that it is a private house, not a palace, and its very strong atmosphere depends on the personality and very long life of Queen Elizabeth.

However there is a point in ending the tour in the Plate Room, because it is a reminder that the house is a working place at every level, from Her Majesty downwards; and each level has its own life, the Household, the Officials, and the domestic staff divided between the Steward's Room and the Servants' Hall. To someone unfamiliar with court life it is a complicated place, quite different from the grandest private house or largest official residence because of the many layers. Unfortunately to explain that properly requires a different book, with photographs of all those involved. It would start with the Household headed by the Lord Chamberlain and the Mistress of the Robes, who appear on state occasions, and the Ladies of the Bedchamber, who appear on national occasions. The regular work is done by the Private Secretary, the Treasurer, the Women of the Bedchamber (who take it in turns to be in waiting), and the Permanent Equerry. Below the Household come the Officials, the Clerk Comptroller, the Information Officer and the Secretariat. The domestic staff is headed by the Steward and Page of the Backstairs, with the Deputy Steward being Page of the Presence. The Pages' titles are the reverse of what an outsider would expect but explained by the 'Backstairs', implying closer contact with Her Majesty. They and some of their colleagues make lightning changes, with footmen's liveries as colourful as the uniforms of the sentries outside.

For much of the time the house is remarkably quiet, with the buzz of London and the life of the Mall over the garden wall seeming far away, except for the marching of the guards and their music that paces out the day, a real-life version of the Pittenweem clock in the Hall. Then, when Queen Elizabeth comes downstairs, the House seems to change gear, and the Steward appears, immaculate in his Page's coat in dark blue with black facings and brass buttons, white tie and medals to announce callers and guests to Her Majesty in the Morning Room or Garden Room . . .

NOTES

– The principal account of the House's history remains *Clarence House* by Christopher Hussey (1949).

– The watercolours of the house in 1861 are catalogued in *The Victorian Watercolours and Drawings in the Collection of Her Majesty The Queen* by Delia Millar (1996).

– The main sources for the contents are a set of Clarence House inventories and a card index in the archives of the Royal Collection.

– There are two articles by the present writer in *Country Life*, 4 September and 11 September 1980.

– Patrick Synge Hutchinson wrote three articles on Queen Elizabeth's collection of Chelsea porcelain in *The Connoisseur Yearbook*, 1958.

– Streatlam Castle was illustrated in *Country Life*, 18 December 1915; Glamis Castle, 9 and 16 May 1947; Gibside, 8 and 15 February 1952; St Paul's Walden Bury, 15 and 22 March 1956.

– *Gibside and the Bowes Family* by Margaret Wills (The Society of Antiquaries of Newcastle upon Tyne, 1995).

– *John Bowes and the Bowes Museum* by Charles Hardy (1970).

– *John Bowes, Mystery Man of the British Turf* by Elizabeth Conran (a booklet published in connection with an exhibition at the Bowes Museum in 1985).

Many of Queen Elizabeth's loans to exhibitions will be found in exhibition catalogues such as that for Paul Nash (Tate Gallery, 1975); Sir William Nicholson (Towner Gallery, Eastbourne and elsewhere, 1995); Matthew Smith (Royal Academy, 1960); Sir David Wilkie (Royal Academy, 1958).

– Some pictures are catalogued in *The Catalogue of Pictures of Her Majesty The Queen*, particularly *The Tudor, Stuart and Early Georgian Pictures* volume (1963) and *Victorian Pictures* (1992) both by Oliver Millar.

Among other useful books on artists and craftsmen are:

– *The Life and Work of Thomas Chippendale* by Christopher Gilbert (1978).

– 'Sir James Gunn 1893–1964,' catalogue of the exhibition at The Scottish National Portrait Gallery, 1964; see also *The Field Marshal 1944–76* by Nigel Hamilton (1986) and Gunn's diary in the possession of the family.

– *J.F. Herring and Sons* by Oliver Brackett (1981).

– *Augustus John: a biography – The Years of Innocence* (1974) and *The Years of Experience* (1975) by Michael Holroyd.

– *For Love of Painting: The Life of Sir Gerald Kelly* by Derek Hudson (1975).

– *Paul Nash, the master of the image, 1889–1946* by Margot Eates (1973) and letter in the Archives of the Tate Gallery.

– Sir John Piper see *Letters/John Betjeman* edited by Candida Lycett Green, Vol. 1, 1994.

– *Edward Seago the vintage years* by Ron Ranson (about 1992).

– *Sickert* by Ora W. Baron (1973).

– *Graham Sutherland: a biography* by Roger Berthoud (1982).

– *Franz Xavier Winterhalter and the Courts of Europe 1830–1870* by Richard Ormond and Carol Blackett-Ord (National Portrait Gallery, 1987).

INDEX OF PERSONS

INDEX